ALLEN COUNTY PUBLIC LIBRARY

FORT WAYNE, INDIANA 46802

You may return this book to any agency, branch,
or bookmobile of the Allen County Public Library.

A Twentieth Century Fund Paper

THE
MEXICAN
TIME BOMB

BY NORMAN A. BAILEY AND RICHARD COHEN

PP Priority Press Publications / New York / 1987

The Twentieth Century Fund is a research foundation undertaking timely analyses of economic, political, and social issues. Not-for-profit and non-partisan, the Fund was founded in 1919 and endowed by Edward A. Filene.

7141747

Foreword

The summer of 1982 is usually considered the beginning of the international debt crisis. That was when Mexico, one of the fastest growing developing countries, was on the verge of defaulting on its debt. In truth, there were many earlier warning signals. Indonesia in Asia, Zaire in Africa, Poland and other East European countries, and Costa Rica all experienced payments difficulties before Mexico ran into trouble. But there is a certain justification for singling out the Mexican debt problem as the real beginning of the crisis. The very size of Mexico's indebtedness, its independence, and its position as one of the leading Latin American countries (as it turned out the international debt crisis was mostly limited to Latin America) made its plight qualitatively and quantitatively different from that of the other countries that had previously encountered difficulty in meeting interest payments on their obligations.

Previous papers in the Twentieth Century Fund series on debt and default have dealt with various aspects of the debt crisis, with debt in Africa, and with the debt problem in specific countries—Brazil and Costa Rica. We have long sought a paper on Mexico, but it took a great deal of time to find a writer who could make a fresh and significant contribution. Norman A. Bailey, a former investment banker and academic specializing in Latin America who was on the staff of the National Security Council from 1981 to 1983 as special assistant to the president and senior director for international economic affairs, has written a paper worth waiting for. With the collaboration of Richard Cohen, author and former publisher of *Washington/World Intelligence Focus,* Bailey has provided an analysis of Mexico's problem and of its significance to other major debtor countries that takes issue with most conventional wisdom on the subject.

v

Bailey is particularly critical of the diagnosis made by the U.S. Treasury, the Federal Reserve, and the international agencies involved in assembling the package of measures designed to rescue Mexico. Because the diagnosis was wrong, Bailey contends, the proffered solution has made things worse rather than better. He points out that by treating the problem as temporary and short term, the treatment has triggered political pressures that threaten Mexico's economic and social stability.

The Bailey-Cohen thesis is both controversial and provocative. But their paper musters an abundance of evidence that the policies Mexico has pursued since the onset of the crisis have done more harm than good. Because of Mexico's proximity to the United States and the many ties and strains between them, what happens in Mexico is, of course, of vital interest to U.S. policymakers. The Baker Plan, named for Treasury Secretary James Baker and announced in October 1985, was a tacit admission that the original prescription was not working. But Bailey contends that the Baker Plan itself deals with structural overindebtedness, which he sees as Mexico's long-term problem, inadequately.

I believe that the Bailey-Cohen paper is a worthy complement to our other work on international debt. We are grateful to the authors for it.

M. J. Rossant, DIRECTOR
The Twentieth Century Fund
January 1987

Contents

1 / Introduction

In October 1985 Secretary of the Treasury James Baker suggested what was billed as a new plan for dealing with the continuing international debt crisis. The Baker Plan, as it came to be known, consisted of three parts, two of which were in fact new. Acknowledging the economic problems underlying the crisis, Baker asked the multilateral lending agencies, the World Bank, the International Monetary Fund (IMF), and the regional development banks, to provide $9 billion in fresh development funds to fifteen debtor countries (nine of them Latin American) over the three years, 1986, 1987, and 1988. These funds were to support domestic growth-oriented reform measures, including liberalization of trade and investment and privatization of state enterprises.

Both of these elements were put forward in explicit recognition of the fact that the debtor countries could not pay if they did not grow. Implicitly, they were an admission that the heroic efforts of the monetary authorities beginning in 1982 to avoid debtor default had neither reduced the debt burden nor permitted enough economic growth for effective management of the debt.

The other part of the Baker Plan was traditional. It called once again upon commercial banks to lend additional money to debtors that would be earmarked for interest payments on existing debt. This measure canceled out much of the promise of the other provisions, so that there was little incentive for debtor governments to participate in the plan and to adopt the politically dangerous reforms that such participation would entail.

What was—and is—wrong with the Baker Plan is not that it provided too little new lending to debtors, as has been charged by many of its critics; to the contrary, it proposed adding substantially to the existing stock of debt of already overburdened debtors. In so doing, it repeated the critical mistake that has characterized the approach of the monetary

1

authorities to the debt crisis since 1982 and accepted the same flawed diagnosis of the crisis undergirding that approach, which is that the debt crisis represents no more than a temporary liquidity shortage, amenable to treatment in the debtor nations by belt tightening to increase cash flow and by the temporary provision of added loans to tide these countries over while adjustment takes effect.

The Third World debt problem is a more profound—and different—problem than that of temporary illiquidity. It is a problem of structural overindebtedness. To be effective, treatment must include debt relief in the form of reduced servicing requirements on the existing stock of debt and, ultimately, a reduction in the absolute volume of debt. Such relief is vital to enable a structurally overindebted economy to sustain economic growth and reduce those deficits which would otherwise require additional borrowing to finance. Without such relief, such debtors can adjust but not grow or grow but not adjust. Either option leads inexorably to the resurgence of the debt crisis.

Mexico, which served as a testing ground for the flawed prescription of the monetary authorities beginning in 1982, provides a case study of the unhappy results generated by the original misdiagnosis.

The First IMF Agreement

Despite the failure of many public officials and the international financial community to credit the news, it was clear during the first half of 1982 that several less developed countries (LDCs), Mexico first among them, were in serious trouble. Concern about LDC debt had been mounting ever since a number of Eastern European and African countries failed to service their debts in 1981 and earlier. Despite these indications, Mexico, which had increased its external debt by $22.4 billion in 1981 alone, was able to borrow another $2.6 billion during the first half of 1982.

In May of that year the International Monetary Group (IMG), an interagency committee of the U.S. government chaired by the then undersecretary of the Treasury for monetary affairs, had met and was warned by the representative of the CIA about an impending Mexican insolvency. The Federal Reserve representative voiced similar concerns, and put forward a proposal to increase IMF quotas and expand the General Agreements to Borrow (GAB) in terms of amounts available as well as by allowing certain LDCs, including Mexico, to participate in the GAB. Treasury officials, who adamantly opposed an IMF quota increase, declared that no crisis existed, and the Federal Reserve's proposal was actually mislaid by the Treasury Department and not taken up by the IMG again until August 12, the very day a desperate Mexican delegation flew to Washington to beg for help to avoid default.

The Treasury was unprepared for the August meetings, which were chaired on the American side by Deputy Secretary of the Treasury Richard T. McNamar.[1] Two billion dollars had to be found by Monday, August 16, if default was to be averted. One billion dollars in food credit from the Commodity Credit Corporation (CCC) was quickly arranged, but despite the urgent pleas of Federal Reserve Chairman Paul Volcker (not a member of the delegation, but haunting the halls) that a settlement be reached on any reasonable terms to avoid a banking panic, the negotiations almost broke down over the discounted price of the $1 billion worth of oil to be purchased by the Strategic Petroleum Reserve. Compromise was finally reached, and over the next four months agreements totaling $8.3 billion also were made with the IMF, the Bank for International Settlements (BIS), the Federal Reserve, and commercial banks.

For its part Mexico agreed to a package of austerity measures that plunged the country into severe depression. According to the IMF, Mexico's adjustment program would lay the foundations for sustainable, noninflationary growth and a return to the international capital markets. According to the de la Madrid government, the Mexican economy was to enter a period of 5 percent average annual GDP growth by 1985, growth which was to last through 1988. What actually happened in the four years that have elapsed from this first rescheduling?

• Mexico's economy has deteriorated, its foreign debt has grown, and its capacity to service its debt has withered and collapsed. The amount of new funds required now is 70 percent higher. Average annual GDP has grown less than 1 percent, average annual per capita income has contracted, the country is $18 billion further in debt, and U.S. exports to Mexico have declined by almost one-quarter from pre-crisis levels.

• As a result of the erosion of the Mexican economy, political forces have arisen which are pressing the Mexican government ever closer to financial default.

• As Mexico, which was once heralded as "the model debtor" because of its strict adherence to the prescription of economic adjustments, has now moved dramatically to reject adjustment, the political consensus that it helped to create for the IMF program for impoverished debtors has unraveled.

The Recent Agreement
So it is ironic that Mexico, reeling from a disastrous earthquake and an even more disastrous decline in the international price of crude oil

(which makes up some 60 percent of its exports), became the first debt-or country to come to an agreement with the IMF along the lines of the Baker Plan, which incorporated the same mistaken remedy of the original program for managing Mexico's debt.

Spurred by the imminent threat of Mexican default and by intense pressure from the U.S. Treasury and Federal Reserve, the IMF agreed to a growth-oriented (though potentially inflationary) package. If fully carried out, it will involve about $4 billion in loans from the IMF, World Bank, and Inter-American Development Bank; $2 billion of U.S. government funds (in the form of export credits and agricultural commodity assistance); and $6 billion of additional commercial bank loans (a portion of which is guaranteed by the World Bank), all by the end of 1987. In return, Mexico agreed to a set of reforms along the lines of the original Baker suggestions, but without a specific timetable for implementation.

Overlooking the fact that the Mexican settlement alone will in just eighteen months absorb more than one-third of the funds that the Baker Plan envisioned being spread among fifteen countries over three years, this latest (and perhaps last) major rescheduling was predictably hailed as yet another "breakthrough" in the debt crisis. It contains some new elements—acceptance by the IMF of the continuation of a large budget deficit by Mexico (10 percent of GDP), suggesting a major retreat from economic adjustment; a (very limited) IMF compensatory funding facility in the event of further declines in the price of oil; and a pledge of additional World Bank and commercial bank funds if economic growth is less than 3.5 percent in real terms in 1987. In their anxiety to stave off Mexican default, the monetary authorities have been forced to retreat from their insistence upon a contractionary economic adjustment. Unfortunately, the main effect of the agreement will be that by the end of 1987, Mexico will owe an additional $12 billion (and the corresponding interest)—while any economic growth it enjoys will have come about largely as a result of unhealthy deficits.

Thus, Mexico's four-year tragedy—a tragedy that has yet to reach its conclusion—provides a case study of the misdiagnosis by the international monetary authorities of the economic disease that struck Mexico and other countries—structural overindebtedness. But even more, it reveals the ineffectiveness of the prescription based on this misdiagnosis. As a case study, it also offers a persuasive argument that decisive domestic political pressure will be brought against governments that are forced to enact prolonged economic adjustments that cut standards of living and borrow yet more money in order to attain a large enough foreign exchange surplus to meet interest payments on their debts. Because it has stood at the cutting edge of debtor-creditor relations since 1982, Mexico offers a unique insight into the evolution of the current phase of the Third World debt crisis.

Mexico stands as an ominous warning. The prescription for resolving the Third World debt crisis promoted by the monetary authorities since August 1982 has failed. In Mexico, where the rescue package was greeted with much hope and showed early signs of success, it proved neither economically nor politically sustainable. The most recent IMF-Mexico deal recognizes the failure of the rescue effort. But the new money promised for Mexico is no more than a desperate effort to stave off Mexican default, and the monetary authorities have been forced to retreat from their insistence upon Mexican economic adjustment.

This turn of events represents a singular twist in the politics of the Third World debt crisis. While regimes in Buenos Aires, Brasilia, and Lima have, since 1983, intermittently waged economic guerrilla warfare to force the IMF and their private creditors to change the orthodox prescription for resolving payments problems, none has succeeded. The political consensus among the international monetary authorities, the Organization for Economic Cooperation and Development (OECD) governments, most private creditors, and some debtors that the IMF formula of more debt and austerity is the correct formula, and the use of this formula in defining the agenda for almost all creditors and debtors, has rested upon one important political factor: the threat of default. The threat that they would otherwise permit default gave the monetary authorities the needed leverage over both private creditors and debtors. Now for the first time Mexico has used the same threat to force the monetary authorities to all but abandon a substantive component of the prescription—debtor adjustment.

As a consequence, the Third World debt crisis has entered a dangerous new phase. While political pressures in Mexico and other debtor nations slowly but perceptibly push them toward default, the orthodox remedy for resolving the crisis is losing credibility and the political consensus supporting it is disappearing.

2 / The Origins of the Crisis

The Mexican debt bomb exploded on a largely unsuspecting international financial community in August 1982. The subsequent psychological shock, combined with the size of Mexico's foreign debt (approximately $80 billion) and the dangerous levels of commercial bank exposure in Mexico, was enough to convince most observers that Mexico's payments problem was unique. Unfortunately, as other large debtors followed Mexico into payments difficulties, the Mexican crisis was looked upon by those observing as the beginning of a serious new threat to international financial stability that quickly became known as the Third World debt crisis. Mexico, as it turned out, was not unique. The subsequent payments problems of other nations did not represent the beginning of a Third World debt crisis but instead a new phase in its evolution.

The Roots

Mexico's crisis evolved over time and in much the same way such crises evolved in other developing nations, especially other Latin American nations. As the 1970s began, Mexico's economy, like that of many other Third World countries, was riddled with profound structural problems created by a fast-growing population and a rapid transition from a rural- to an urban-based economy with wide disparities in class and regional income.

From 1940 to 1970 the Mexican economy grew at an average annual rate of 6 percent—equal to that of such dynamic economies as Japan, West Germany, South Korea, and Taiwan. In addition, during the 1950s and 1960s Mexico coupled economic growth with an inflation rate that averaged less than 5 percent, while many of Latin America's other large economies were suffering intermittent hyperinflation.[1]

But thirty years of exemplary growth accompanied by a low rate of inflation masked enormous structural stresses—stresses that were aggravated by the distribution of Mexico's post-World War II wealth and the means by which this new wealth was created.

7

Mexico's economy had been traditionally marked by wide disparities in income according to socio-economic class and geographic area. These wide income differentials, typical of poverty-ridden Central American economies, were exacerbated by the postwar concentration of new industry in the country's already more prosperous central and northern urban centers and by the sustained depressed wage levels of the country's work force—both rural and urban—during this period. In a 1980 report, the World Bank identified Mexico as having one of the worst profiles of income distribution of any nation.[2]

By the middle of the 1960s the rapid growth of Mexico's population, averaging 3.5 percent a year, was generating a second structural problem—chronic unemployment and underemployment. Mexico's postwar development strategy served to exacerbate the problem. By concentrating on rapid industrialization and capital-intensive job creation, the economy increasingly lagged in providing enough jobs for the staggering number of new entrants into the labor market each year. At the same time, efforts at rapid industrialization encouraged a huge rural migration to Mexico's cities; Mexico City, Guadalajara, and Monterrey, the major centers of industrial concentration, soon became overpopulated with the unemployed and the underemployed. The potential political threat to Mexico's stability posed by these growing structural problems began to attract the attention of the nation's policymakers. Nevertheless, Mexico's governing elite failed to give priority to them until the political order exploded in 1968 with student-led demonstrations.

In response, Mexico, like many other developing nations, began expensive development programs aimed at reducing economic and demographic stress. These programs required very large capital investment, which to a great extent determined Mexico's economic policy in the 1970s. The economies of the developing countries were constructed to take advantage of the prevailing global inflation. Cheap foreign sources of capital carrying low to negative real interest rates in the advanced industrial countries encouraged foreign borrowing, while rising commodity prices encouraged rapid exploitation and export of commodities such as petroleum—and the belief that a large foreign debt could be efficiently serviced into the indefinite future. Growing export revenues and inexpensive foreign money made expensive development programs appear financially sound.

Obsessed with its sovereignty in light of its economic weakness, especially in relation to the United States, Mexico found debt a politically preferable option to direct equity investment. For much the same reason, the major countries of Latin America took the same route; very few developing countries, Taiwan is the best example, chose the path of equity investment.

Thus, the increased borrowing by Mexico (and many other commodity exporters with huge development needs during the decade of the 1970s) using inexpensive foreign loans as the vehicle for economic development, and the eager advancing of credit by commercial banks with almost no regard to the risks involved, eventually brought about the 1982 crisis.

The Role of the Lopez Portillo Regime

The dramatic economic imbalances caused by the efforts of Jose Lopez Portillo's administration (1976-82) to quickly redress entrenched structural problems, especially Mexico's demographic time bomb, proved the final straw. Economic development policy pursued by the Lopez Portillo government was drafted and supported by technocrats who came to dominate the Mexican governing elite in the second half of the 1970s. Its program rejected the methods adopted by the previous administration (Luis Echeverria, 1970-76) to deal with the problems of income disparity and demographic stress. Relying more upon traditional techniques for social control associated with the ruling Partido Revolucionario Institutional (PRI), Echeverria had drastically increased government welfare programs and urban services to take account of the needs of the growing numbers of urban poor and launched a new land reform effort aimed at increasing rural employment opportunities.[3]

To finance these programs while still aggressively promoting continuation of the postwar development strategy, the Echeverria regime had been forced to incur large foreign debts—debts which by 1976 Mexico could no longer afford to service. Difficulties generated by the 1976 payments crisis, which forced Mexico to seek IMF and U.S. government financial help, were compounded by the failure of Echeverria's effort to defuse the political effects of Mexico's structural problems.

When technocrats of Lopez Portillo's government took over, they defined a new economic policy that sought to attack the problems at their source. Mortgaging Mexico's newly developed oil wealth and, in effect, the future of the Mexican economy, the government contracted huge new foreign debts to finance an unprecedented reindustrialization targeted at creating substantially greater numbers of jobs in the industrial and construction sectors.

Lopez Portillo's Industrial Development Plan of 1979, which evolved into the all-inclusive Global Development Plan, defined the technocrats' vision of Mexico's economic future. Premised on continued rapid economic growth and a more even dispersal of industry throughout the country,[4] the objective was to reduce overpopulation in Mexico City and other urban centers and thus reduce the long-term costs of welfare and service programs.

By the end of the 1970s Mexico's exploding population meant 700,000-

800,000 new entrants to the job market each year. Simply to produce positive per capita GDP growth, the Mexican economy would have to grow by more than 3 percent annually. But to add sufficient jobs to support new labor market entrants, it would have to grow in real terms by at least 7 percent annually.

Faced with these difficult economic and demographic conditions, the government of Lopez Portillo sought to generate a dramatic economic leap that would propel the Mexican economy beyond politically dangerous structural problems. From 1977 through the first months of 1981 it appeared that the government's efforts might succeed. While Mexico was exploiting and exporting its hydrocarbon wealth, world oil prices rose dramatically.[5] Cheap sources of foreign money resulting from low to negative real U.S. interest rates in the second half of the 1970s encouraged borrowing. Mexico reached average annual levels of growth of 8 percent from 1978-81, and the initiation of the Global Development Plan brought with it a huge boom in construction jobs during 1980-81; between 1980 and 1982 four million new jobs were created.

The costs of this impressive growth and job creation were new and profound economic imbalances that were the telltale signs of a disease which had already blighted a number of African and Caribbean nations in the middle 1970s—structural overindebtedness. The disease is not of a short-term, temporary nature, so its cure is neither easy nor quick; it requires a radical remedy, one which can work a cure only over time.

A Growing Malady

As for the symptoms of the disease, from 1978 to 1982 Mexico came to depend on large and growing fiscal deficits to directly finance its development strategy and to provide its social safety net comprised of large subsidies for food and fuel. By 1982 the fiscal deficit as a percentage of GDP had reached 17.6 percent, an unprecedented level. Mexico's private sector became the government's junior partner in the development plan; it adopted a buy now, pay later policy.

At the same time, Mexico's development strategy relied on massive imports of capital goods. The large fiscal deficits and the maintenance of an overvalued peso generated a significant rise in consumer imports. An abnormal part of Mexico's average annual growth during the 1978-81 period then became dependent on large fiscal deficits and rising imports.

Believing that it could sustain its fiscal spending and huge import bill through growing exports of petroleum and the rising price of those exports, the Mexican government sanctioned a massive investment in the hydrocarbon sector. From 1978 to 1982 petroleum revenues quickly became an expanding share of all government revenues and the overwhelming share of Mexico's exports. Mexico's fiscal and trade deficits grew with the enormous growth in petroleum output and export. Yet imports outstripped Mexico's expanded exports in part because non-oil exports remained stagnant, a reflection of the noncompetitive nature of the country's manufacturing sector.[6] Under Lopez Portillo, nothing was done to increase the competitiveness of domestic industry; in fact, the private sector was increasingly dominated by the public sector and protected from foreign competition.[7]

To pay for its fiscal and trade deficits, Mexico resorted to growing domestic and foreign borrowing. Foreign debt, which amounted to $33.9 billion in 1978, grew to $87.6 billion by the end of 1982. Mexico's private and public deficits were partially financed by a ballooning domestic debt, which in turn fueled the growth of inflation from a 17.5 percent annual rate at the end of 1978 to 98.8 percent at the end of 1982.

By 1978 the barometer of Mexico's ability to service its foreign debt, its debt service ratio (annual debt service divided by exports), was already 87.3 percent—an unprecedentedly high level.

By 1980 growth had become structurally dependent on borrowing. In fact, Mexico's structural overindebtedness had become so severe that unless it continued to expand the rate of growth of domestic and foreign borrowing, it would be unable to sustain its fiscal and trade deficits. As borrowing increased, so did Mexico's debt service requirements—adding an organically essential expense that could be paid only by accumulating even larger debts (see Table 2.1).

Two developments taking place in the early 1980s, which reflected the transition of the global economy from the inflationary 1970s into the disinflation of the 1980s, spelled the beginning of the end for the attempt by the technocrats to transform the Mexican economy. These developments brought Mexico to a state of aggravated overindebtedness. U.S. real interest rates skyrocketed in 1981, with the U.S. prime rate reaching 21 percent. As a result, Mexico's interest payments on its huge foreign debt soared, especially since an increasing proportion of the country's debt was tied to floating interest rates (see Table 2.2). Against this backdrop, Mexico's debt service ratio and interest-to-export ratio shot up as its ability to service its debt sharply deteriorated.[8]

Then, in the fall of 1981 the contraction in world trade, resulting from the onset of global recession, slowed demand for petroleum. At the same time, non-OPEC producers continued to increase oil production, leading to a drop in price and a slowdown in the growth of Mexican oil exports. Mexico's capacity to service its foreign debt weakened further.[9]

Throughout 1981 and the early months of 1982 the rapid decline of Mexico's international payments capacity was alleviated by foreign creditors who continued to make large new loans to Mexico. But it was not long before rumors about Mexico's precarious financial condition

Table 2.1
MEXICO'S SYMPTOMS OF STRUCTURAL OVERINDEBTEDNESS 1978-1982

		1978	1979	1980	1981	1982
FISCAL DEFICIT*	—as % of GDP	4.9%	6.1%	6.7%	12.2%	17.6%
TRADE DEFICIT ($ billions)**	—Exports	$6.1	$8.8	$15.1	$19.4	$21.2
	—Imports	$7.9	$12.0	$18.8	$23.9	$14.4
	—Current Account	-$2.7	-$4.9	-$7.2	-$12.5	-$6.2
CRUDE OIL EXPORTS VS.	—Crude Oil Exports	$1.9	$4.0	$10.4	$14.6	$16.0
NON-OIL EXPORTS ($ billions)**	—Non-oil Exports	$4.2	$4.8	$4.7	$4.8	$4.8
GOVERNMENT'S ROLE IN THE ECONOMY*	—Expenditures as % of GDP	22.8%	24.3%	26.9%	30.6%	28.2%
	—Revenues as % of GDP	23.5%	24.6%	30.0%	26.0%	30.2%
DEBT AND THE ABILITY TO PAY IT**	—Total Disbursed External Debt ($ billions)	$33.9	$40.2	$50.7	$74.9	$87.6
	—Debt Service Ratio	87.3%	105.0%	70.6%	98.8%	152.6%
	—Interest Payments-to-Export Ratio	22.1%	22.8%	22.0%	27.2%	44.2%
	—Debt-to-GDP Ratio	290.9%	247.2%	203.2%	243.1%	302.0%

* From Secretaria de Programacion y Presupuesto.
** From Chase Econometrics.

Table 2.2
MEXICO'S VULNERABILITY TO HIGHER INTEREST RATES

	1978	1980	1982
TOTAL DEBT WITH FLOATING INTEREST RATES ($ billions)	$19.9	$32.2	$59.3
PERCENT OF TOTAL DEBT WITH FLOATING INTEREST RATES	60%	70%	78%

Source: Chris C. Carvounis, *The Debt Dilemma of Developing Nations* (Westport, Conn.: Quorum Books, 1984), p. 9.

began to circulate among domestic and foreign investors—rumors which, when acted upon, weakened the country's ability to service its foreign debt still further.

Rising inflationary pressures led domestic investors in the private sector to lose confidence in the Mexican economy. Because the government refused to devalue the peso, it precipitated fears of a future larger devaluation, and stimulated a round of capital flight out of Mexico. As much as $36 billion left Mexico from 1976 to 1982—a good portion of it in 1981 and 1982.[10]

Foreign investors then began to lose confidence in the Mexican economy, and as a result, new loans were available only on a short-term basis at very high rates of interest. From the beginning of 1981 to the August 1982 payments crisis, Mexico borrowed $25 billion (increasing its foreign debt by close to 50 percent to finance its deficit), most of it short-term—a pattern that would cause the country's debt service ratio to show astronomical growth in 1982-83.

At the end of 1981 the Mexican government had been forced to acknowledge the necessity of adjusting its deficits, implementing (minimal) import restrictions, and cutting its budget. But the Lopez Portillo regime feared the political consequences of adjustment far too much to engineer a drastic reduction in the fiscal deficit along with a substantial cutback in its imports. As the crisis began to grow, the government took somewhat stronger action in February 1982, when a mini-devaluation of the peso was enacted in an effort to reduce imports, increase non-oil exports, and restrain capital flight.

But the structure of the Mexican economy was too fragile to be saved by mere gestures. In April fears about the extent of the economic crisis emerged when Alfa, the Monterrey-based industrial group which had been one of the strongest performers on the Mexican stock market, announced it was suspending payments on $2.3 billion of its foreign debt.

In an attempt to control the growing crisis, the government announced a broad adjustment program, authored by Finance Minister Jesus Silva Herzog.[11] Within three months it became clear that the Lopez Portillo government had no stomach for the potential political and social consequences of Silva Herzog's adjustment program. By that time both the fiscal deficit and inflation were rising rapidly.

Mushrooming deficits and inflation once again terrified domestic savers. Fears of a maxi-devaluation of the peso, precipitated in part by clumsy government moves in the direction of exchange controls, led to an estimated $9 billion in capital flight in early August. At the same time, Mexico's foreign creditors also began to panic, cutting off lines of credit. The result was a rapid rundown of the country's international reserves—a situation similar to that faced by Echeverria in 1976—and a full-blown payments crisis.

Mexico Was Not Alone

The symptoms of Mexico's structural overindebtedness—like the structural problems that had compelled the Mexican government to accept the risks and make the gamble it did in the 1970s—were evident in the economies of many developing nations, especially those of the Latin American nations in 1981-82.

Mexico's huge fiscal and trade deficits were paralleled by those in Argentina and Brazil. Mexico's large and growing debt-to-GDP and debt service ratios also were mirrored widely, especially among Latin American debtors. Of these debtors, only Brazil was not deeply reliant on commodity exports and the stability of commodity prices, and only Brazil, by following an export-led development strategy, had constructed a relatively competitive manufacturing sector. But Mexico also was not alone in running higher inflation rates and building sizable domestic debt in the early 1980s; both Argentina and Brazil surpassed Mexico in those areas. Finally, aside from Brazil, capital flight was rampant throughout Latin America, especially in such large debtor nations as Argentina and Venezuela (see Table 2.3).

The deep, underlying structural pressures of a rapidly expanding population, widespread urban overpopulation, and inordinate unemployment and underemployment were also evident in Brazil, Argentina, and Peru. And though Mexico may have exhibited the symptoms of structural overindebtedness with perhaps more intensity than any other Latin American large debtor, middle-level debtor Peru and small debtor Bolivia were considerably more structurally impaired. Mexico differed only because she was not burdened by the major expense assumed by many other Latin American governments—a large defense establishment.

Table 2.3
MEXICO WAS NOT ALONE

		Brazil	Venezuela	Argentina	Mexico
DEBT SERVICE RATIO (Debt Service/Exports)	1981	106.8%	76.5%	139.5%	96.8%
	1982	143.5%	98.5%	164.1%	152.2%
CURRENT ACCOUNT ($ billions)	1981	$-11.9	$4.0	$-4.7	$-12.5
	1982	$-16.3	$-4.2	$-2.4	$-6.2
INFLATION (CPI)	1981	100.6%	11.0%	28.7%	104.4%
	1982	101.8%	7.3%	98.8%	164.8%
PERCENTAGE OF MANUFACTURED GOODS EXPORTS TO TOTAL EXPORTS	1981	46.0%	4.0%	20.0%	14.0%
	1982	47.0%	4.0%	21.0%	14.0%
CAPITAL FLIGHT ($ billions)*	1976-82	$3.00	$25.00	$27.00	$36.00

Source: Chase Econometrics.
* From Morgan Guaranty Trust Company.

Still, Mexico's debt crisis of 1982 did not mark the beginning of the contemporary phase of the Third World debt crisis. The 1981-82 recession sparked a wave of payments crises which began in Eastern Europe and spread to Peru and Bolivia prior to reaching Mexico in August 1982.[12]

What in fact defined the Mexico payments crisis as a watershed in the late summer of 1982 and afterward was the psychological shock it delivered to the international financial community, to creditor governments, to commercial banks and, through the media, to the populations of the OECD and debtor nations. It was the panicky reaction of the commercial banks to the eruption of Mexico's payments crisis that brought home to the rest of the world that Argentina and Brazil exhibited negative economic symptoms strikingly similar to those afflicting Mexico. The resulting cutoff of voluntary lending to those economies precipitated, as it had for Mexico, serious payments crises. The rapid succession of Argentine and Brazilian debt crises on the heels of Mexico's fostered the appearance that a new phenomenon had emerged that threatened to seriously damage the world financial system—a Third World debt crisis.

Only in the subsequent unfolding of Mexico's debt crisis and its management did a unique element emerge. Mexico—more than any other debtor—followed faithfully the prescription offered by the international monetary authorities for curing its financial difficulties. While Mexico kept to a strict regimen of domestic adjustment from the beginning of 1983 to the middle of 1984, Peru and Bolivia quickly found such adjustments politically and economically unsustainable, Argentina resisted it, and Brazil quickly abandoned it. Mexico's ability to pursue adjustment over a prolonged period resulted from a second unique characteristic, its political system.

3 / The Costs of Misdiagnosis

When in August 1982 the Mexican crisis invaded the boardrooms of commercial banks along with the offices of the IMF, the Federal Reserve, and the U.S. Treasury, it was clear that only urgent action could forestall a default. The U.S. government came through with close to $3 billion, including $1 billion in agricultural financing from the CCC, $1 billion as prepayment for the purchase of oil for the Strategic Petroleum Reserve, and $925 million in a short-term bridge loan from the Federal Reserve. The European central banks, functioning through the BIS, also came up with a short-term bridge loan of $925 million. In addition, OECD governments pledged Mexico about $2 billion in export credits.

But all this was no more than financial mouth-to-mouth resuscitation aimed at keeping the patient financially functional in the short term while longer-term solutions were devised. The same forces that pulled Mexico back from the brink—the IMF, the Fed, and the Reagan administration—took responsibility for finding a way to end its economic distress.

The trouble was that the would-be saviors trying so desperately to help did not understand the nature of Mexico's underlying problems. They assumed that they were treating a short- to medium-term liquidity shortage, rather than an aggravated case of structural overindebtedness. They also erred in assuming that developments in the world economy during that period would aid the Mexican economy; in fact, the global economic environment from 1983 to 1986 served only to exacerbate its problems. And they also misjudged Mexico's internal political situation. These errors of judgment meant that the rescue package that they put together was flawed. Instead of helping Mexico, it triggered an adverse reaction that helped push the Mexican government toward default.

Underestimating the Mexican Economy's Structural Weakness

Because the monetary authorities misdiagnosed Mexico's economic disease as a liquidity shortage, they resorted to a traditional cure, which was derived from an IMF prescription used in the 1950s and 1960s to correct short-term balance of payments problems. It called for the assumption of new debt to finance the servicing of old debt. Then, when debt service appeared inordinately large in the 1980s, the monetary authorities proposed that the component of debt service comprising principal be rescheduled. In addition, the debtor country would be required to undertake economic adjustments to reduce its trade and fiscal deficits and to restrain domestic money growth and inflation.

This formula had been successfully applied at a time when national economies operated under the discipline of the Bretton Woods monetary system (which did not tolerate extreme structural imbalances such as unmanageable fiscal and trade deficits or excessive inflation), and when the imbalances of national economies could be controlled with relative ease. The abandonment of the Bretton Woods system in the early 1970s set the course for a decade of global economic instability, characterized by rising rates of inflation, excessive fiscal and trade deficits, and structural overindebtedness.

An overindebted economy such as Mexico's depends on fiscal and trade deficits—and thus on an expansion of its debt, both foreign and domestic—for an inordinate proportion of its economic growth. If the Mexican government had limited the growth of domestic debt and took on only enough foreign debt to pay interest, thereby bringing about a rapid reduction of trade and fiscal deficits as recommended by the monetary authorities, severe and painful shocks to the Mexican economy would have resulted.

That is what happened. Aggravated by the initiation of adjustment in 1983, Mexico's domestic recession turned out to be much deeper than expected. Projections of Mexico's GDP growth for 1983 had ranged from -2 to -4 percent; instead, Mexico's GDP contracted by more than 5 percent. Mexico's 1984-85 growth rate, which averaged 3.75 percent, was in part predicated on resort to fiscal expansion and money supply growth prohibited under the terms of the adjustment program. If Mexico had abided by its adjustment targets, it is probable that the economy would have experienced negative average per capita GDP growth in 1984-85. The large contraction in personal consumption and investment during the 1983 depression never fully recovered during the inflationary growth of 1984-85, creating a major disincentive for domestic and foreign investors to risk new investment in Mexico. As a result, it would be well beyond 1985 before Mexico could produce positive per capita GDP growth.¹ All of these developments were not anticipated by the international authorities who were treating Mexico.

In addition, even when Mexico's economy was free of the effects of government reflationary policies in 1983 and 1984, the adjustment that led to unanticipated weakness in growth also failed to reduce inflation to anticipated levels. In each of those two years inflation was reduced by only 50 percent of what had been projected, suggesting that to bring inflation down to targeted levels, Mexico's 1983 depression would have to have been still deeper and longer than it was.

According to the orthodox prescription, the reduction of Mexico's twin deficits and its inflation rate to acceptable levels could have been achieved only if the economy had endured a prolonged state of semi-depression conditions. Alternatively, Mexico could have abandoned the prescribed path and *reflated* (which is precisely what it did during 1984 and 1985) in order to grow at rates higher than the rate of population growth. There was a third—untried—option: Mexico could have resumed positive per capita GDP growth without resort to inflation if it had been granted significant debt relief.

Mexico's debt-to-GDP ratio actually grew during the span of the adjustment program. If the IMF's remedy had been effective, the ratio would have declined. In 1982 Mexico's debt-to-GDP ratio was 49.4 percent. From 1983-85 it averaged 56.2 percent, a figure that would have been even higher if Mexico had not resorted to reflation. In 1986 the Mexican GDP will contract by 4 to 5 percent, while, under the terms of its new agreement with the IMF, it will add to its foreign debt. Therefore, Mexico's debt-to-GDP ratio will be even higher in 1986 than it was during 1983-85.

Thus, over the course of the new programs, Mexico's overindebtedness has actually become more acute. Moreover, the overindebtedness could have been reduced if Mexico had only been granted effective debt relief from the inception of its adjustment program.

Overestimating the Positive Impact of the Global Economy

Overindebted developing sector economies are especially vulnerable to periods of global deflation, such as Mexico experienced in 1981-82, when real interest rates are high and commodity prices depressed. In 1982 the monetary authorities projected changes in the international economy that would have permitted Mexico to better service its debt while reducing the burden on its domestic economy. Their forecast called for a global recovery, lower real interest rates, and steady to rising commodity prices. While a world recovery emerged in 1983, its structure served to limit the support it provided to economies such as Mexico's.

Global recovery, moreover, began to slow down by the middle of 1984, much more than had been anticipated. Mexican exports grew by only 7.8 percent in 1984, the peak of the recovery, and then contracted by 12.8 percent in 1985. Mexico was not alone in its inability to make headway during the global recovery. Exports grew by 11 percent in 1984 for Latin America's eight largest debtors, including Mexico, but 66 percent of the growth was attributable to one country, Brazil, which had followed a different development strategy. In 1985 the exports of these same debtor economies contracted by 7 percent.

As a result, Mexico's debt-to-export ratio, which would have declined under the IMF-projected global economic conditions, continued to grow from 1983 to 1985. In 1982 its debt-to-export ratio had been 302 percent; from 1983 to 1985 it averaged 308 percent.

Instead of the anticipated global economic environment, what has emerged is a world economy marked by downward pressure on commodity prices and high real interest rates. The dramatic drop in oil prices that began in early 1986 had the effect of thrusting a visibly shaky Mexican economy into a new depression. It also brought a sharp fall in Mexico's exports and thus impaired its ability to finance its interest payments on external debt. Moreover, by reducing government revenues, it sent the fiscal deficit as a percentage of GDP into double digits. In fact, since exports have collapsed and (under the terms of the IMF agreement) foreign debt is growing, Mexico's 1986 debt-to-export ratio, like its debt-to-GDP ratio, will be much greater than that registered from 1983-85.

Political Miscalculations

International financial authorities did more than engage in a misdiagnosis of Mexico's economic troubles. They also misdiagnosed the political capacity of the country to sustain adjustment. The economic misdiagnosis led to an underestimation of the economic dislocation and increasing overindebtedness that resulted from a prolonged and painful contraction. The political misdiagnosis led the authorities and creditors to either ignore or be insensitive to the pressures exerted on the Mexican government to abandon adjustment.

The rise of Mexico's nationalist left to positions of authority in the Lopez Portillo government in 1982 troubled the international financial community. But it was the sudden nationalization of Mexico's private banks, announced by Lopez Portillo on September 1, 1982, that terrified foreign creditors by raising the specter of a Mexican moratorium or default on its foreign debt. When the nationalist left and Mexican trade unions were suppressed under the new administration of President Miguel de la Madrid in December and their opposition to adjustment contained, the mood shifted from excessive pessimism to excessive optimism. The fact that Mexico was prepared to try to sustain a difficult economic adjustment did not mean that it was on the road to recovery.

Despite the prolonged domination of Mexican politics by the PRI, changes in Mexico's political order have been taking place over the past twenty years. The power of the nationalist left, the labor unions, and what might be described as an "Old Class" centered about the bureaucrats of the PRI and associated labor union leaders has been weakening. A "New Class" of technocrats—most educated in the United States and Western Europe and representing a younger generation with little or no experience in the PRI—has replaced the Old Class as the dominant political force in Mexico's government elite since 1976.[2]

While technocrats have risen to positions of influence in many other Latin American countries, they have not won the political power that they have enjoyed in Mexico. The polities of all other Latin American nations are either competitive democracies or military dictatorships. In these political environments, technocrats function under the policy prescriptions of alternating political parties or military juntas. Mexico's political structure, though, is unique. One political party, the PRI, dominates government, representing the interests of often conflicting elements of the national elite and exerting vast social control through PRI-linked popular organizations. The PRI-aligned trade unions, of which the Confederation of Mexican Workers (CTM) is the most powerful and well-organized, is still a force to be reckoned with. But by gaining dominance over other institutional centers of power in the party, the PRI central and regional structure, as well as the CTM, the New Class has won control of the government, the seat of institutional power.

The Old and New Classes are separated by major social, cultural, and political differences. True to the Mexican political system, however, they operate within a governing elite that draws a sharp political line between itself and outsiders such as the opposition National Action party (PAN) and the Catholic Church. The New Class is especially concerned about its own and Mexico's image in the outside world, particularly in the United States and the international financial community, while the Old Class is relatively unconcerned about how it is regarded by foreigners; it is more interested in maintaining domestic power for itself and its immediate domestic allies.

The differences on issues are sharp between the Old and New Classes. On debt, the New Class has made a priority of maintaining good relations with the international financial community by servicing its debt. In contrast, the Old Class is ready to accept default if servicing debt creates domestic political hardship for the PRI. On domestic economic

policy, the New Class is most interested in rapid industrial moderniza-
tion and is prepared to reduce traditional patronage to achieve it. The
Old Class, on the other hand, seeks to hold domestic power at all costs,
preserving the patronage system and resorting to vote fraud, a tactic
deplored (though sometimes accepted as necessary) by the New Class.

The split between the two groups is a reflection of a political dilemma that confronted the Mexican elite in the early 1960s. The popular
organizations of the PRI—labor, peasant, and professional—began to
atrophy so that they gradually lost much of their influence and effectiveness in exercising social control.[3] Efforts at self-reform and modern-
ization were modest. The Old Class, fearing a loss of power, blocked
and undercut reforms. Nevertheless, reform and technocrats both gained
a foothold. The ascension of Lopez Portillo to the presidency in 1976
was a turning point. Lopez Portillo was the first Mexican president to
have virtually no party experience. His regime dropped the populist
rhetoric of the traditional PRI and cautiously sought to open the electoral process to other political parties. Most important, during the tenure
of Lopez Portillo, the centers of Old Class power—the party structure
and the popular organizations—were severely weakened.

From 1976-82 the Mexican labor movement lost much of its power
and influence.[4] Workers' wages suffered, strikes were suppressed, union
membership declined. The PRI peasant organization—the National Confederation of Peasants (CNC)—was all but eliminated, and the PRI's
populist land reform policy was suspended.[5] The government sought to
lessen the growth of urban welfare programs, thereby downgrading a
major political plank of the PRI and the nationalist left. In addition,
the Lopez Portillo government antagonized segments of the PRI's nationalist left by adopting an increasingly accelerating export program
for Mexico's hydrocarbon sector in the face of protests that Mexico would
thus become hostage to the U.S. market.[6]

Miguel de la Madrid, Lopez Portillo's successor and a technocrat
educated at Harvard, continued to favor the New Class. De la Madrid
named members of the Old Class to only minor cabinet positions, suppressed strikes with even more vigor than had Lopez Portillo, purged
elements of the nationalist left and labor from previously held positions,
and launched a major anti-corruption campaign which, if fully carried
through, would have fallen heavily on the Old Class.

This process of political transformation had several important consequences. It significantly weakened those groups of the governing elite,
the nationalist left and labor, who were the most ardent opponents of
economic adjustment and least concerned with maintaining Mexico's
image and credit rating abroad. But by downgrading the patronage
machine of the PRI's popular organizations and abandoning the rhetoric

of populism, the New Class weakened the vitality and the usefulness of traditional mechanisms for generating mass support for the government and for social control. The credibility and legitimacy of the New Class and the government rested on the effectiveness of government development strategy and the adequacy of a social safety net.

The result was that if adjustment caused the collapse of the development strategy and brought an end to price subsidies, the Mexican government's ability to politically sustain adjustment would be badly damaged. If that were to happen (as it later did), the New Class would be under pressure to abandon adjustment from a number of sources: a loss of mass support that would result in political isolation and an erosion of legitimacy; the increasing frustration and anger of the newly consolidated middle class whose rising material expectations would be dashed; and, ultimately, an effort by the Old Class to take advantage of the government's weakness to regain power.

The Plunge Toward Default

The responsibility for Mexico's structural overindebtedness and its payments crises lies with the Lopez Portillo government. It gambled on Mexico's economic future, and lost. That gamble was supported by a willing accomplice—private creditors who continued to underwrite Mexico's debt even when the risks were evident. But the responsibility for misdiagnosing Mexico's economic and political condition and then urging a faulty cure lies with the monetary authorities—the IMF and the central banks of the industrialized democracies. What turned out to be a wrongheaded prescription for curing Mexico's ills eventually led to economic and political circumstances that would have forced almost any conceivable Mexican government to abandon support for the solution.

The de la Madrid government therefore became an increasingly unwilling accomplice of the monetary authorities and private creditors. Faced with a sharp erosion of material conditions with little to no prospect of improvement and under political pressure from both inside and outside government, the de la Madrid administration later took concrete actions such as reflation to revive the economy and relieve political pressure. These actions increased the risk of a default, but by the middle of 1984 the government was prepared to accept such a risk.

Mexico's relationship with its foreign creditors underwent a fundamental transformation after the August 1982 payments crisis. The terms by which the nation's enormous foreign debt problems were to be managed were no longer matters to be solely decided by the Mexican government. Instead, they would be negotiated between the government and a group of foreign institutions—including multilateral lending institutions, foreign governments and their central banks, and foreign private creditors whose ultimate priorities often sharply differed from those of the Mexican government. The new dynamic, with its evident political overtones, affected the interests of important domestic Mexican constituencies and thus brought them into the new political equation.

Following the payments crisis of 1982 the IMF, the Federal Reserve Board, and the Reagan administration made avoiding Mexican default the overriding objective of Mexican debt management. Washington was anxious because default was a threat to the integrity of the international financial system and the U.S. banking system. The Mexican government and its private creditors also had a very strong interest in avoiding default—but this goal was not as all-encompassing for them as it was for the international and national monetary authorities and the U.S. government.

These differences in the extent of the commitment to avoiding default among the major participants involved in the Mexican crisis gave rise to serious disagreements. The IMF, the Federal Reserve, and the Reagan administration were totally against default. That was not the case for either the Mexican government or some of its private creditors. The procedure used to manage Mexico's debt since 1982 has rested on the stability of the new political dynamic involving the government of Mexico, Mexico's foreign creditors, and affected domestic constituencies. This stability requires that none of the negotiating parties resort—or be forced to resort under political pressure—to default. But the way Mexico's debt has been managed over the past few years has increasingly undermined stability, building economic and political pressures that are themselves driving Mexico toward default.

4 / Mexico the Model

That a dynamic hurling Mexico toward default was built into the program for managing Mexico's debt held great importance for the politics of the Third World debt issue. Mexico's position at the forefront of the evolving line of action in debtor-creditor relations was recently confirmed by Federal Reserve Chairman Volcker. Upon his return from a hush-hush trip to Mexico City in June 1986, a concerned Volcker warned two congressional committees that while the U.S. banking system could withstand the shock of a Mexican default, such an action could quickly encourage other hard-pressed debtors, including Argentina, Venezuela, Ecuador, and Nigeria, to go the same route. Volcker's anxiety over Mexico's role in the latest phase of the international debt crisis was far different from the praise he lavished upon Mexico during the first stage of the crisis. In 1982 the Mexican government had, after a show of resistance, taken a cooperative attitude in negotiations with the monetary authorities. Its willingness to accept the IMF prescription for resolving the debt crisis was instrumental in generating a consensus among creditors that Mexico was a model debtor. Certainly, the Mexican model set the ground rules for treating other troubled debtors, in particular, Brazil and Argentina. Because of its special role in defining the course and content of debtor-creditor relations, Mexico was to play an equally critical role in precipitating the breakdown of the consensus.

The initial consensus on the appropriate prescription for dealing with the debt crisis was established in an atmosphere of high risk for all of the principal players—the Mexican government, Mexico's private creditors, and the international monetary authorities. Something close to panic prevailed in Mexico City, where high-placed officials could see no way out of the crisis, and among the executives of banks in Europe and the United States, who had no desire to throw away good new money in an attempt to save all of their old bad loans. Ultimately, the power of the international monetary authorities to contain the panic and restore

25

order resided in their determination to confront the commercial banks and the Mexican government with an ultimatum: the only way to prevent default and its consequences was by cooperative action. If the commercial banks and the Mexican government did not reverse course and join forces under the leadership of the international authorities, then default, with all of its frightening ramifications, could not be avoided.

Forging the Creditor Cartel

But it was a near miss. While the monetary authorities feared a chain reaction, the commercial banks completely ignored this risk, and in a panic, decided to stop lending to Mexico and other Latin American debtors. Their decision was encouraged in part by the belief that the international monetary authorities would not permit Mexico and other debtors to go bankrupt.

The panicked rush out of voluntary lending by the banks to troubled Third World debtors signaled the opposition of private creditors to playing the roles assigned to them in the proposed plan by the international monetary authorities for resolving Mexico's debt problem. The banks balked at providing fresh loans so that insolvent debtors could service their debts. Their cutting off of voluntary lending to Mexico spread to other debtor economies during the fall of 1982, creating an even greater threat to the security of both the U.S. banking system and the international banking structure, of which the major U.S. banks formed so large a part.

In a high stakes showdown with Mexico's private creditors, the international monetary authorities—the IMF, the Federal Reserve, and the European central banks supported by the Reagan administration[1]—hung tough. After weeks of cajoling Mexico's private creditors, IMF Managing Director Jacques de Larosiere summoned them to a meeting in New York in November 1982. There, he informed them that they either come up with $5 billion in new loans or the IMF would refuse to act to stabilize Mexico's foreign debt. De Larosiere insisted that the IMF would not offer Mexico $3.7 billion in new credits over three years (as expected), nor would it define—or pressure Mexico into acceptance of or compliance with—a new adjustment program.

De Larosiere's ultimatum carried a time limit of one month. By mid-December the banks would have to agree in principle to new financing of $5 billion for Mexico as well as to a rescheduling of Mexico's short-term debt. The same day that de Larosiere issued his warning, Volcker, who was speaking in Boston, backed up de Larosiere's position. Volcker argued that a Mexican default represented a clear danger to the integrity of the international banking system, so that all measures necessary to avoid it were justified. Hard on the heels of these statements, central bankers of the OECD countries applied pressure on their commercial banks to reverse course and come to the rescue of Mexico to avoid future default.

The efforts of the monetary authorities were largely successful. Concerted action was taken. But the forging of unity among the creditors was only skin deep. Differences between the monetary authorities and the commercial banks and among the commercial banks themselves soon came to light. Although the banks provided the $5 billion called for by the IMF and agreed to reschedule Mexico's short-term debt, their fear of lending to the debtor countries was not allayed. The banks virtually shut down voluntary new loans to the debtors. They put up funds only at the insistence of the monetary authorities and even then, only in amounts sufficient to finance debt service. Such lending could hardly be called voluntary. While the monetary authorities exerted pressure on the banks to increase lending, the banks resisted, intent on limiting their exposure to the loans already on their books.

There were also differences among commercial banks. United States regional banks—relatively new arrivals in the sovereign Third World debt business and with less exposure, and thus less to lose, than the money center banks—put up the strongest resistance to the pressure of the monetary authorities[2] (see Table 4.1). European and Japanese banks, more willing than their U.S. counterparts to reduce current profits to build up loan loss reserves against bad Third World debt, also proved more resistant to pressure from the monetary authorities. Thus, the consensus supporting the IMF formula for Mexico and other debtors was far from solid.

Pressuring Mexico

The resistance of Mexico's creditors soon found its counterpart in Mexican resistance to the prescription for adjustment called for by the IMF.

For more than five-and-one-half years, Lopez Portillo had overseen a transition of power in the Mexican governing elite from the Old to the New Class. In the process, his government's legitimacy and popularity came to depend on the success of a grandiose and expensive economic development strategy. When that development strategy collapsed with the emergence of the debt crisis in August 1982, forcing the Mexican government to ponder a future of austerity and joint management of its economy with the international monetary authorities, no single Mexican felt the political shock more than Lopez Portillo.

To counteract the economic and political chaos around him, Lopez Portillo sought allies in the PRI's nationalist left and in the bureaucrats of the Old Class. He conspired with the nationalist left behind the backs of his own cabinet during August, formulating a plan to nationalize Mex-

Table 4.1
THE REGIONAL BANKS HAD LESS TO LOSE
THAN THE MCBs IN MEXICO'S DEBT
(Exposure of U.S. Banks in Mexico Relative to Capital)
(% End Year)

	1977	1978	1979	1980	1981	1982
NINE LARGEST U.S. BANKS	32.9%	30.4%	29.6%	37.8%	44.4%	44.4%
ALL U.S. BANKS	27.4	23.4	23.0	27.6	34.3	34.5

Source: U.S. Federal Reserve Board of Governors, "Country Exposure Lending Survey."

ico's banks. Lopez Portillo blamed the payments crisis on the banks, alleging that they were responsible for aiding and abetting the flight of capital from Mexico.[3]

In nationalizing the banks and appointing left-wing nationalists to critical positions (led by Carlos Tello's appointment as director of the Central Bank of Mexico), Lopez Portillo shocked his allies of the New Class, along with Mexico's private sector and the international financial community. His action unleashed what at the time appeared to be the forces in the country's governing elite identified as being most opposed to yielding to international and especially American pressure, and least opposed to the alternative of a Mexican default.[4]

This point was clear in the polarization, evident within the Lopez Portillo administration since late 1981, over whether to enact adjustment, and if so, to what extent. Finance Minister Silva Herzog (who would tender his resignation with the bank nationalization only to have it rejected by Lopez Portillo) emerged as the leading advocate of adjustment. The nationalist left and its leading spokesman, Jose Andres de Oteyza, minister of National Patrimony and Industrial Development, and the labor movement, remained ardent opponents of anything more than the most minimal adjustment.[5]

During the negotiations between the IMF and Mexico in the fall of 1982, the international monetary authorities sought to dispel Mexican illusions that the creditor nations and their private banks had no choice but to come to Mexico's rescue because of their large exposure in Mexican debt and also because of the threat to the United States posed by economic decline and unrest in Mexico. The authorities argued that unless Mexico accepted adjustment far more severe than that proposed by the Mexican government, there would be no deal; already in deep recession for lack of foreign exchange, Mexico would have to fend for itself. In view of the hard line taken by the banks, it could not expect a bailout.

Despite Lopez Portillo's resistance and the opposition of the nationalist left, the Mexican government had no real option. While hoping that the terms of adjustment sought by the monetary authorities could be moderated, President-elect Miguel de la Madrid and the mainstream of the New Class were of no mind to confront the financial powers. Ultimately, neither was Lopez Portillo. The advance of the nationalist left in the government was followed by a retreat. Technocrats and friends of private bankers were appointed by the government to run the nationalized banks. In December 1982 the government accepted an IMF adjustment program of austerity that was far from Mexico's original bargaining position, and very close to the IMF's original position.[6]

Consensus Consolidated

At the September 1983 IMF-World Bank annual meeting, Mexico, the focus of fear and scorn one year before, was again the focus. This time Mexico was hailed as a symbol that the Third World debt crisis could now be managed, so long as other debtors followed the Mexican model. The IMF embarked on a public relations campaign that exaggerated the successes of Mexico's adjustment. According to an IMF report on Mexico's 1983 economic performance, "the new administration [of de la Madrid] which took office on December 1, 1982, moved quickly and decisively to implement the adjustment program."[7]

It is true that by the end of 1983 Mexico had reached many of its adjustment targets. Most important, the fiscal deficit, which was to have been reduced from 17.6 to 8.5 percent of GDP in 1982, was reduced to 8.7 percent—very close to the target. The Mexican government drove up interest rates and contained money supply growth. January wage increases were set at 25 percent and, even when added to a 15.5 percent additional increase in June, the growth in wages fell far below the 80 percent rate of inflation. Mexico abandoned the strict exchange controls put in place in August 1982, permitting a sizable devaluation of the peso. Imports contracted by 41 percent, and a $6.2 billion current account deficit was turned into a $5.3 billion surplus. And Mexico's capital flight all but stopped as the financial category of errors and omissions, which had grown by $11 billion in 1982, grew by only $400 million in 1983.

Equally important, the government of Mexico had succeeded in defeating those national forces most strongly opposed to austerity—the nationalist left and the labor movement. All key cabinet positions in the de la Madrid government were filled by technocrats; Tello was replaced at the central bank and Silva Herzog was retained as finance minister. In January the government announced its intention to introduce a number of liberal economic reforms inimical to the nationalist left and the labor movement.

The adjustment program had been fully implemented in 1983, bringing in its wake a significant increase in unemployment and underemployment and a dramatic drop in living standards. These trends put pressure on the CTM and other trade unions to do what they could to cushion or reverse the impact of adjustment. After threatening a general strike in June, Fidel Velasquez, the head of the CTM, backed down from a direct confrontation. Velasquez demanded a 50 percent wage increase (still below inflation) but was firmly rebuffed. Turning to less confrontational tactics, Velasquez and the CTM made no greater headway. Independent unions opposed to the PRI confronted the government in June and July, but they too were rebuffed.

Wage settlements were arrived at on a factory-by-factory basis, and as soon as nominal wage raises were agreed to, the government would nullify them through reductions in price subsidies. The net result was a weakening of both the established labor movement and labor unions in general. The political decline of the CTM was highly visible as the number of labor deputies in the PRI congressional contingent was reduced and labor appointees were noticeably absent from government positions traditionally held by labor unions. Finally, de la Madrid personally wooed conservative independent trade unions.

From 1983 through the middle of 1984 relations between the de la Madrid government and the international monetary authorities remained friendly. A clublike atmosphere existed among the senior officials of Mexico's finance ministry and central bank and the IMF, the Federal Reserve, and the group of thirteen banks that formed the steering committee of Mexico's private creditors. Mexico sat at the developing line of action between debtors and creditors, defining new terrain in the relationship. In early 1984 the monetary authorities, spearheaded by Volcker, sought to gain private creditor support for an unprecedented rescheduling aimed at reducing the debt servicing pressure on Mexico during the life of its adjustment program. After gaining the support of the bank steering committee, the rescheduling, replete with a marginal reduction in interest rates and a multi-year rescheduling of principal payments, was consolidated in the first half of 1985.[8]

As a testimonial to its supposed financial resuscitation and as a demonstration of its commitment to the integrity of the international financial system, Mexico joined Venezuela and Brazil in issuing a short-term bridge loan to an insolvent Argentina in March 1984. While some observers among Mexico's creditors saw in this gesture the dangerous beginnings of Latin America-wide debtor unity, it delighted the international monetary authorities. They regarded it as a welcome sign of debtor responsibility, putting pressure on creditors to be more forthcoming in the case of Argentina, and encouraging Argentina to recognize the virtue of striking a deal with its creditors.

5 / The Consensus Unravels

Even while Mexico was being promoted as the model for other debtors to follow, trouble was brewing. Mexico's unique political system and the domestic political transformation that had taken place over a decade impaired the power and influence of the nationalist left and the labor movement. They could not stop or even impede the austerity measures that were part and parcel of the economic adjustment program. But this was not the case among other Latin American debtor nations, except perhaps in Chile where the military suppressed the labor movement and the left (but in Chile, unlike in Mexico, a political consensus—that is, social peace—does not exist). Among the more structurally impaired and smaller debtors such as Peru and Bolivia, the first stroke of adjustment sparked widespread left-labor agitation and the dramatic collapse of popular support for the government. Large debtors such as Argentina and Brazil, with fragile new democracies and powerful nationalist left and labor movements, rejected and quickly abandoned austerity.

The Mexican crisis reemerged in mid-1985, when it became apparent that Mexico, the model debtor of 1983-84, was now a model failure. In the summer of 1984, the Mexican government decided to break its agreement with the IMF and abandon its adjustment targets. In response, the IMF first warned that it would halt loans to Mexico, and then, one year later, stopped its lending. In June 1986 the once model debtor turned around and threatened the monetary authorities and its private creditors with default unless it was given debt relief and permitted to reflate.

Inexorably, the misdiagnosis of Mexico's ills and the subsequent wrong-headed prescription for them by the monetary authorities caused new problems. Once again, Mexico was headed toward default. Once on this route, Mexico spearheaded the unraveling of the consensus supporting the IMF and provoked an unprecedented retreat by the monetary authorities.

31

Why Mexico Broke with the IMF

In the fall of 1984 the Mexican government lowered interest rates and allowed domestic money supply to grow noticeably beyond the targets established by the IMF. At the same time, the government began to increase spending, causing the fiscal deficit to edge above the IMF target. These moves reflected the government's decision to reflate the economy; its decision was taken with the knowledge that by doing so, Mexico would be violating its agreement to abide by the IMF's adjustment program.

What led the Mexican government to take such a risk—especially when, as the favored model of the monetary authorities, it was in the process of negotiating an unprecedented restructuring of its foreign debt? The commonly held explanation was that the Mexican government, facing two important gubernatorial elections in Sonora and Nuevo Leon in mid-1985, believed that the only way to maintain its dominant position was to reverse its economic course by easing up on austerity. That explanation, though, was at best superficial. Political reasons were behind Mexico's decision to breach its agreement with the IMF, but the July elections in themselves were not the motivation. A president of de la Madrid's character—an extremely cautious technocrat who had great admiration and respect for the international banking community—would not risk everything for two governorships in northern Mexico.

In fact, pressure on the de la Madrid administration came from three political directions in mid-1984. From outside the government, the frustrated urban middle class, increasingly leaning toward the right-wing PAN, posed one threat. Internally, the Old Class within the PRI, the party organizers, the labor union leaders and their political supporters, sought to regain some of their lost power and influence. Perhaps the most potent challenge to the popularity and legitimacy of the New Class came from the disaffected but silent masses—urban workers, housewives, and the unemployed, along with the peasants. Unwilling to join the opposition, they were no longer prepared to support either the PRI or the government.

The cause of the pressure was clear. Although the Mexican government enjoyed the backing and praise of "outsiders"—foreign creditors—for its willingness to embrace adjustment, the Mexican people suffered. The economy was shaken by a deep depression, far deeper than anticipated in 1983, and the recovery in the first half of 1984 was disappointingly modest. Personal consumption declined by 7.5 percent in 1983, total investment by 27 percent, and public investment by 32 percent. Unemployment shot up to 15-16 percent, and underemployment to close to 30 percent. At the end of 1983 almost half of the Mexican labor force was either unemployed or underemployed. Real wages collapsed in 1983, and by 1985 had fallen by close to 50 percent. The decision to reflate during 1984-85 did not make up for the losses suffered in personal consumption or investment and made no dent in unemployment and underemployment (see Table 5.1).

Table 5.1
MEXICO: THE CRASH OF '83
(In Percentage Points of Growth)

	1980	1981	1982	1983
GDP	8.3%	7.9%	-0.5%	-5.3%
GDP PER CAPITA	5.3	5.2	-3.1	-7.7
PERSONAL CONSUMPTION	7.5	7.3	1.1	-7.5
INVESTMENT	14.9	14.7	-15.9	-27.9
GOVERNMENT INVESTMENT	16.7	15.8	-14.2	-32.5
IMPORTS	31.9	20.3	-37.1	-41.7

Source: Chase Econometrics.

The Mexican government, dominated by the New Class since the oil boom of the late 1970s, had gained power and popularity because it had provided growth, jobs, and subsidies for the urban masses. The success of the New Class had also weakened the PRI's traditional organizations, which had depended in large part on their control over patronage. In the 1983 depression, growth, jobs, and price subsidies all evaporated and the fallout began to hit the de la Madrid regime harder than it hit its opposition within the PRI. The government sought to buy time by depicting adjustment and depression as a short but necessary interlude that would enable the economy to start growing again at a rapid rate. The government's ability would ultimately rest on whether it could make good on de la Madrid's 1983 promise of 5 percent annual real growth from 1985 through 1988.

By the summer of 1984 the de la Madrid regime acknowledged its predicament. In his second State of the Union address, de la Madrid appealed to the silent masses, conceding that the process of economic recovery had not yet been felt "to any appreciable degree in the daily lives of individuals and families." He went on to admit that inflation is "still extremely high, growth is slow," and sympathized with the "distress of housewives trying to stretch the family budget." Accordingly, the government took the risk of reflation.

The deterioration in public confidence in the government became all too evident when an unusually high 49.5 percent of eligible voters failed to participate in the July 1985 elections for which the PRI and the government had mobilized. Then, in his third State of the Union address in September 1985, de la Madrid had to admit that his reflationary economic policies had failed and Mexico had to return to severe adjustment. The the government's credibility suffered further deterioration later that same month when, following the massive earthquake that hit Mexico City, government rescue and cleanup efforts were widely perceived to have been mishandled. In Mexico City de la Madrid was denounced as a lame duck, one without any support at the grass roots level. The regime's growing political isolation was signaled when de la Madrid was publicly booed by his countrymen at the opening of the world soccer championships in 1986.

The government also had to face a direct challenge from the frustrated urban middle class, especially from those residing in the states bordering the United States. The 1983 depression had shattered their rising expectations, and led them to blame the government for everything that had gone wrong.[1] The regime's political difficulties in the north first surfaced in the local elections of July 1983. The rightist PAN stunned the government, winning twelve mayoral contests with the support of the urban middle class vote.[2] The electoral shock served to further increase tensions within the PRI between the New and Old Classes. The victories by "outsiders" spurred the PRI's party machine to resort to massive vote fraud in subsequent elections.

Large-scale vote fraud has characterized all important elections from 1984 through 1986. But even with that assistance, the PRI's share of the vote contracted significantly in the more prosperous regions and in the five largest cities. In the 1985 elections the ruling party recorded only 45 percent of the tabulated vote in Mexico's five largest cities (its percentage of the real vote in Mexico City, Guadalajara, Juarez, Monterrey, and Netzahualcoyotl was probably closer to 35 percent), further confirming the extensive slippage in middle-class support for the PRI and government.[3]

Even though the labor movement and Old Class were defeated with the ascension of de la Madrid in 1983, they still held significant power in the PRI bureaucracy and labor movement. While avoiding direct confrontation with the New Class, the party machine and the labor union leaders defended their centers of power, often mounting successful rearguard actions against government efforts at political and economic liberalization. Of greater significance, the PRI organizations had become more important to the de la Madrid government in the elections. This was especially the case in the July 1986 gubernatorial elections in Chihuahua.[4] With the contest to succeed de la Madrid already under way, the support of the Old Class has become critical for the various contenders, leading to a revival of sorts for the party bosses.

By the middle of 1984 the New Class and the de la Madrid cabinet were faced with a rising challenge to adjustment. This challenge kindled debate within the cabinet, resulting in a political split. Silva Herzog championed the orthodox austerity policy against Minister of Planning and Budget Carlos Salinas de Gortari, who, sensitive to political pressures, argued for a more confrontational approach to the debt issue that would, at a minimum, help restore popularity and legitimacy and mollify the Old Class, and perhaps stop the deterioration in the economy that was so harmful politically.

Above the debate was President de la Madrid. As one of the architects of the New Class's development strategy, he was inclined to oppose confrontation. But as a member of the PRI, he also was anxious to ease his government's political bind. So he steered a middle course, avoiding direct confrontation while attempting to stimulate the economy. Thus, against Silva Herzog's advice and yet unwilling to break openly with Mexico's creditors, de la Madrid breached Mexico's agreement with the IMF and began to reflate.

Adjustment Abandoned

By the end of 1984 Mexico's reflation could not be concealed. The abandonment of the IMF's adjustment targets was clear to both public and private creditors. During the first half of 1985 the IMF and the U.S. government urged the de la Madrid government to return to austerity. But once the agreement with the IMF was breached, the cooperative, even intimate, atmosphere that had characterized Mexico's relations with the IMF, the U.S. government, and its private creditors soured.

Silva Herzog, who had lost in the earlier cabinet debate, tried to restore the relationship. He got the government to agree to contain growth of money supply in early 1985 and, following the July elections, announced fresh efforts to restrain the growth of Mexico's fiscal deficit and reduce imports. But these maneuvers proved to be too little too late.

Mexico's resumption of inflationary growth had enormous costs. Although GDP grew by 3.5 percent in 1984 and 4.0 percent in 1985, that amounted to barely positive growth on a per capita basis. Meanwhile, the symptoms of the original disease—structural overindebtedness—were exacerbated. In 1984 Mexico's fiscal deficit was 6.2 percent of GDP, exceeding the target of 5.5 percent and making clear that the government had not fared as well in meeting its target as it had the previous year. Independent observers, moreover, estimated the fiscal deficit to be even higher—in the range of 7.0-7.7 percent of GDP. The original fiscal deficit target for 1985 of 3.5 percent of GDP was revised upward, to 5.1 percent. Nevertheless, the government's expansionary fiscal policies caused the fiscal deficit to reach 9.6 percent of GDP.

Money supply was loosened in 1984 to accommodate the new expansion (see Table 5.2). Money supply had risen by 41.1 percent in 1983; the following year it rose 63.1 percent. In 1985, with restraint allegedly in force once more, the increase was 60.0 percent, breaking its target (see Table 5.3). As a result, inflation, which had been slated to increase by 35 percent in 1985, actually grew by 65 percent (see Table 5.4).

Table 5.2
MEXICO MISSES ITS FISCAL TARGETS

	1983	1984	1985
FISCAL DEFICIT TARGET AS % OF GDP	8.5%	5.5%	3.5%
REVISED FISCAL DEFICIT TARGET AS % OF GDP	—	—	5.1
ORIGINALLY REPORTED GOVERNMENT DEFICIT AS % OF GDP	8.7	6.2	9.6
REAL GOVERNMENT FISCAL DEFICIT AS % OF GDP	8.7	7.0-7.7*	9.6

Source: Banco de Mexico, *Informe Anual*, 1984 and 1985.
* Bailey-Cohen estimate and *Informe Anual*.

Table 5.3
MEXICO'S MONETARY EXPANSION OF 1984-1985

	1981	1982	1983	1984	1985
PERCENTAGE GROWTH OF M-1	32.8%	61.9%	41.4%	63.1%	59.6%
PERCENTAGE GROWTH OF MONEY MULTIPLIER M-1	-8.0	-16.9	-10.8	5.7	14.8

Source: Chase Econometrics.

Imports, which had contracted in 1982 and 1983, grew by 21 percent in 1985; exports, largely because of the downward pressure on oil prices, contracted by 15 percent. Thus, Mexico's 1984 trade surplus contracted by 42 percent in 1985, and its current account surplus of $4 billion turned into a $500 million deficit. The worsening structural factors underlying Mexico's overindebtedness—a rising fiscal deficit, a reduced trade surplus, declining oil prices, and rising inflation—when combined with an overvalued currency forced a fresh round of capital flight in the spring and summer of 1985. As a result, Mexico's international reserves contracted by 46 percent in 1985.

Table 5.4
MEXICO'S RENEWED INFLATION

	Annual Change	Monthly Change
JANUARY 1984	73.4%	6.4%
FEBRUARY	73.3	5.3
MARCH	72.3	4.3
APRIL	69.1	4.3
MAY	67.4	3.3
JUNE	67.1	3.6
JULY	64.5	3.3
AUGUST	62.8	2.8
SEPTEMBER	62.7	3.0
OCTOBER	63.0	3.5
NOVEMBER	59.2	3.4
DECEMBER	59.2	4.2
JANUARY 1985	60.8	7.4
FEBRUARY	59.0	4.2
MARCH	58.4	3.9
APRIL	56.5	3.1
MAY	55.1	2.4
JUNE	53.4	2.5
JULY	53.7	3.5
AUGUST	56.0	4.4
SEPTEMBER	57.6	4.0
OCTOBER	58.0	3.8
NOVEMBER	59.8	4.6
DECEMBER	63.7	6.8

Source: Banco de Mexico, *Indicadores Economicos.*

In August 1985 Mexican government officials were reporting the inescapable outcome of resort to inflationary growth—an imminent new payments crisis. Spokesmen for the Finance Ministry said $4 billion in "new money" was needed to stave off default in 1986.

The inevitable result of Mexico's resort to inflationary growth was a stern message from the IMF on September 19, 1985, the very day of the earthquake that struck Mexico City. The IMF's Board of Governors found Mexico to be out of compliance with its adjustment agreement and announced that $900 million in credits still remaining in the Extended Fund Facility for Mexico would not be disbursed. Now, in addition to having fallen into renewed payments difficulties, Mexico was in open conflict with the IMF.

Although Mexico had hoped to avoid a break with the monetary authorities and its creditors by being careful not to explicitly threaten default, its policy of reflation nevertheless represented an implicit recognition that it was prepared to risk default. Its actions did not go unnoticed abroad. To the contrary, the break with the Fund and its sudden impending insolvency sent a shock wave through the international financial community second only to the shock experienced at the onset of the crisis. It was clear that the crisis was still very much alive for many debtors, including Mexico.

Latin America's debtors had been holding formal discussions on their problems since 1984 through the so-called Cartagena Group. The Cartagena discussions centered on the forging of a common front in dealing with their creditors and other ways in which they might gain increased leverage in debt negotiations. Despite all their talk, unity proved elusive. Instead, a few countries acted on their own. By unilaterally limiting Peru's debt service payments to a fixed percentage of exports, the populist government of Alan Garcia defied its creditors. Brazil, piling up a huge trade surplus and therefore not in dire need of new loans, frequently avoided austerity by running up massive domestic debt and inflating. Venezuela had long averted making a deal with the IMF, preferring instead to deal separately with its private creditors. Bolivian finances were in a total shambles.

Of the structurally overindebted South American nations, only Ecuador and Chile showed some durable commitment to IMF-determined adjustment, with Chile often flirting with noncompliance. Argentina, the most recalcitrant debtor of 1983-84, became the new model for those desperately trying to revive the credibility of the old and failing orthodox prescription in mid-1985. But the Argentine currency reform undertaken to cope with the devastation to the nation's economy caused by Argentina's previous dependence on inflationary growth did not represent a commitment by the Argentine government to the old IMF prescription. The so-called "Austral Plan" sought to deal with the underlying inflationary social dynamic that has traditionally plagued the Argentine economy by promoting wage-price controls and restraining the domestic budget deficit, and tying these measures to a drastic currency reform.

The Baker Plan

The unraveling of the consensus based on the Mexican model, along with the declining leverage of the monetary authorities over debtors, played a part in launching the Baker Plan, which to some degree, aimed at restoring a consensus by modifying the old formula. The monetary authorities, led by the Federal Reserve, the IMF, and the World Bank, all endorsed the Baker Plan in the fall of 1985, with the Fed lobbying strenuously for acceptance by both private creditors and debtor governments. The reactions of creditors and debtors alike demonstrated how far the consensus had disintegrated and how much influence the monetary authorities had lost.

The loss of leverage over the creditors could be attributed to the increased risk associated with loans as the capacity of debtors to service debt deteriorated, and to the decline in the ability of the monetary authorities to get debtors to accept and carry out effective adjustment programs. In addition, the decline in interest rates that began in 1985 and the stricter loan loss reserve requirements imposed on banks in the United States resulted in a buildup of bank capital and reserves against suspect Third World loans. (European banks had began building up large loan loss reserves earlier.) Banks were therefore better insulated against the effects of defaults on existing debt and more fearful of extending new loans. Meanwhile, debtors were finding the political penalties associated with adjustment increasingly onerous, which in turn led them to consider as palatable actions that might risk default.

From its inception, the Baker Plan made concessions to deteriorating creditor unity by practically excluding U.S. regional bank participation. It did so in the belief that the regional banks would provide an obstacle to the plan's acceptance—and an excuse for U.S. money center banks and European and Japanese banks to opt out. Even with heavy lobbying, highlighted by Paul Volcker's appearance at the annual meeting of the American Bankers Association in fall 1985 (where he renewed his warning, repeated successfully since the fall of 1982 that unless new money were put up, default would be inevitable), the commercial banks have not pledged the money asked of them in the Baker Plan.

As for the debtors, Mexico, with its economic need for new financing in 1986 and its evident political need for economic growth, was considered the logical candidate for the role of first debtor country to be subject to the liberalization provisions of the Baker Plan. When the Mexican government showed little real interest, the spotlight turned on Argentina, but Argentina showed no immediate interest either. Finally, the plan's promoters had to settle on small debtor Ecuador as the potential first recipient—but so far, nothing has materialized.

Standstill

In the case of Mexico, there was something approaching paralysis. The Baker Plan's failure to make headway was not the only setback. Progress in restoring Mexico's finances and getting it to once again adjust its swollen imbalances was nonexistent.

In the wake of the IMF decision to freeze the Extended Fund Facility disbursements, William Rhodes, chairman of the Bank Advisory Group on Mexico, was still arguing that Mexico would get new voluntary loans, though most of Mexico's creditors considered he was indulging in wishful thinking. Most observers believed that Mexico's private creditors would not meet the nation's request for $2-3 billion in private bank loans for 1986 and that to get new money, Mexico would have to accept a renewal of strict austerity.[5]

While the Baker Plan paid lip service to the need for growth, the IMF, one of its principal supporters, insisted that Mexico return to austerity as the price of a new stabilization package and the provision of new loans to forestall bankruptcy. The IMF's offer embroiled the government of Mexico in an intense internal debate over how much it should or could afford to accept in terms of new adjustments. Undoubtedly, it would have been in the country's best interests to come to a quick agreement with the IMF, regaining access to credits and avoiding a fresh capital flight. Politically, though, the prospect of a new round of belt tightening was unacceptable to some members of the government, leading to prolonged debate and delay.

There were increasingly divergent views in the cabinet about what policy to adopt. One faction was opposed to giving up growth even if it was accompanied by inflation. Silva Herzog and Salinas de Gortari clashed anew.[6] The proposed 1986 budget reflected the conflict, suggesting the president's extreme caution along with his reluctance to enter into a direct confrontation with the monetary authorities. The budget, which called for the fiscal deficit to be slashed from 9.6 to 4.6 percent of GDP in 1986 and forecast zero growth as well as a reduction of inflation from 65 to 45-50 percent, seemed to be premised on several questionable assumptions. It was an exercise in tightrope walking, presenting just enough commitment to restraint to appease the monetary authorities at the same time that it sought to limit the negative impact of adjustment on growth.[7]

Toward a New Balance

The devastating earthquake that hit Mexico City was a social, psychological, and economic blow. It also greatly increased resentment of the government. Yet the shock to the country caused by the disaster was marginal when compared to the sudden and sharp drop in world oil prices that began in February 1986. Many observers have equated the two events, regarding them as natural disasters responsible for the new Mexican depression and the crippling of Mexico's finances in 1986.

But the oil shock was hardly a natural disaster; it was the inevitable result of the powerful global deflationary forces that have dominated the 1980s. What is more, the twin disasters of 1985 and 1986 did not by themselves bring the Mexican economy to its knees; they only accelerated the process, a process that was apparent throughout 1985, and that observers should, in fact, have recognized.

What the decline in the oil price did was to present the Mexican cabinet with a stark set of economic circumstances, and their grave political consequences, that demanded a decisive and immediate response. In a more dramatic way than in 1981-82, when global deflation first aggravated Mexico's economic disorder, the price decline of 1986 traumatized the nation's economy and finances despite the ameliorating effects of declining U.S. interest rates.[8] The Mexican economy, which had been projected to show zero growth in 1986, will contract by 4-5 percent; inflation, which was to decline to 45-50 percent, will climb to 100 percent, the country's trade surplus will evaporate, and the current account will run significantly in deficit. As a result of the major loss to government revenues, the fiscal deficit as a percentage of GDP has already shot up to 13 percent.[9] At the same time, Mexico's ability to service its debts has collapsed and its debt service, debt-to-export, and debt-to-GDP ratios have all grown substantially.

As the zero growth austerity budget of 1986 had stirred intense debate within the de la Madrid cabinet only months before, the already thin support for the Silva Herzog position evaporated as Mexico faced a fresh depression. The entire cabinet—including Silva Herzog—realized that the adjustment targets set up in the budget for 1986 had become unthinkable. Attempts to reduce fiscal and trade deficits would only deepen the new depression.

The de la Madrid government had to answer two questions: What help did Mexico need to weather the new crisis? And how could it be obtained? Identifying what Mexico needed was relatively easy; how to get it was a different matter entirely. It was quickly decided that the country would not cut its fiscal deficit to anything near the 6.0 percent of GDP proposed by the IMF. In addition, to finance external debt service obligations Mexico would need more than the $4 billion originally projected, and since it was likely that Mexico's finances would continue to be hurt even if oil prices recovered somewhat, it would also need increased amounts of new loans in the future. If Mexico was to gain some shelter from the vicissitudes of global deflation, then the volume of new loans available to it would have to be linked to the value of its oil exports. And Mexico needed debt relief—its yearly debt service payments had to be reduced to reflect the losses in its earnings from exports.

But the Mexican government could not reach internal agreement on how bring this about. Conflicting rumors emanated from Mexico City as to what the regime's tactics would be. Many delegates to the Punta del Este meeting of the Cartagena Group in March of 1986 assumed that the Mexicans would lead a campaign for debt relief. But no such campaign materialized. The reason was that the cabinet was split, with Salinas de Gortari proposing confrontation with creditors over debt relief and Silva Herzog—who was in constant discussion with Volcker, Baker, and the IMF during this period—favoring negotiations.[10] De la Madrid was in the middle, eager to stimulate the economy but hesitant about directly challenging the international banking community.

Since the IMF had not indicated flexibility on its proposed adjustment targets, the paralysis in the government meant that it had the worst of both worlds, with neither growth in the economy nor help from the IMF. The economy in the first quarter of 1986 was extremely weak, and pressure was building on the peso. Rumors from Mexico City to the effect that the government would resort to unilateral action to get its way merely inflamed the pressure on the peso. As June began de la Madrid gave credence to these rumors when he publicly charged creditors with choking Mexico to death.[11]

A shift in tactics had occurred. For the first time a major international debtor—under growing internal political pressure as a result of the aftershocks of prolonged adjustment and aggravated overindebtedness—took the club of default into its own hands and applied it to the monetary authorities and its private creditors. Once the Mexican threat was fully appreciated, the monetary authorities—also for the first time—retreated on almost every outstanding issue, all but conceding on the questions of adjustment, of promoting a large two-year loan package for Mexico, and of supporting a small compensatory funding facility to shield the country from the impact of oil price fluctuations. No concession was made, though, on the critical issue of debt service relief.

Volcker's visit to Mexico City last June 9 was provoked by credible rumors coming out of Mexico that the de la Madrid government was on the verge of unilateral action. While propaganda after the visit hinted that all had been solved and that a new IMF-Mexico deal was imminent, Volcker's testimony on Capitol Hill revealed his deep concern over the prospects of a Mexican default. And both Volcker and Baker were alarmed enough over Mexico's intentions to launch a lobbying effort to get the IMF to soften its adjustment demands.[12] Although the mid-June ouster of Silva Herzog was largely the result of his opposition to a new round of Mexican reflation, his removal had a profound psychological impact on Washington and Wall Street.[13] The belief that Mexico might be serious about taking unilateral action to reduce its debt burden surfaced anew. Then, in late June Washington received information that the Mexican cabinet, with de la Madrid present, had just endorsed the creation of a facility that would hold interest payments in escrow in peso accounts if Mexico's international revenues did not increase.[14]

The new finance minister, Gustavo Petricioli, an individual with none of the independence or ambition of Silva Herzog, joined the president in insisting that Mexico be permitted to grow by 3-4 percent in 1987-88 —a level that would represent a return to the growth of the 1984-85 period. Petricioli immediately went to Washington, where he presented the IMF, Volcker, and Baker with a list of demands for linking Mexico's debt to oil earnings and for a new method of calculating the Mexican fiscal deficit that would, in effect, understate it.

By early July the IMF and the U.S. government were prepared to make more concessions, forming the basis of agreement between the IMF and Mexico on July 22. Under the agreement, Mexico's fiscal deficit target for 1986 would be 10 percent of GDP. In addition, the IMF agreed to accept a new method for calculating the deficit, which may understate it by another 2-3 percent of GDP, and to support Mexico's 1987-88 growth targets of 3-4 percent as well as press private creditors to create a special support fund that would supply additional money to Mexico if oil prices fell to between $5-9 a barrel for ninety days during the next nine months. (Mexico would pay money into the fund if oil prices rose above $14 a barrel for ninety days.)

This retreat by the monetary authorities, along with the changes in the relationship between debtors and creditors that dates from the summer of 1985, is tantamount to the dissolution of the old understandings that had been in effect since the end of 1982. But no clear new rules of the game have emerged to replace the ones that were dissolved.

6 / What Must Be Done?

The recent agreement along the lines of the Baker Plan between the IMF and Mexico offers insight into a dramatic change in Mexico's relationship with its creditors, one which demonstrates the rapidly eroding leverage of the monetary authorities. It also demonstrates the growing incentives for default among debtors. But the agreement is not a remedy for Mexico's economic problems; the problems will worsen.

Already suffering from acute structural overindebtedness, Mexico will not have any of its foreign debt retired under the agreement. To the contrary, Mexico will be adding another $12 billion to its foreign debt as a result of its new accord with the IMF, increasing its foreign obligations. The arrangement also represents a virtual abandonment of the policy of adjustment and, in essence, endorses Mexico's reflationary policies of 1984-85. Whatever ad hoc measures the government might put in place to prevent capital flight, Mexico's inflationary plan, which is essential if the economy is to grow by the targeted 3-4 percent in 1987-88, combined with larger fiscal and current account deficits, will stimulate a resumption of capital flight, and at some point result in a new set of Mexican payments problems necessitating yet a further expansion of foreign indebtedness.[1]

In addition, the arrangement will do nothing to alleviate the domestic political pressures that are driving the Mexican government toward default. The political challenge may be temporarily slowed, but it will not be reversed. Indeed, it can be expected to regain momentum with the growth of inflation. So the pressures on the government make it inevitable that Mexico's relations with its creditors will remain troubled.

By resorting to the threat of default, Mexico achieved almost all of its stated objectives. But though it could claim a victory in its negotiations with the IMF, Mexico failed to achieve the essential ingredient of an actual solution to the country's debt problems—debt relief. Only with debt relief can Mexico reduce its deficits and resume noninflationary growth.

45

Without debt relief, the Mexican debt crisis is bound to continue. At some point in the not too distant future, Mexico will again have to resort to threatening default to win new concessions from its creditors. But Mexico's private creditors proved very reluctant to approve the current IMF agreement with the threat of default hanging over their collective heads, and it is far less likely that they would endorse a future package.

Far from being a victory or a solution, the current Mexican agreement signals a critical new phase of the international debt crisis. The incentive to default rises as Mexico and other debtor nations face renewed payments crises and faltering economic growth resulting from either adjustment or inflation. At the same time, political stability, which is essential for avoiding default, has been subject to increasing stress.

What is abundantly clear is that the leverage of the monetary authorities over debtor governments has withered. Peru and other countries have taken unilateral action. They have gotten away with it. Mexico's threat of default forced a retreat by the IMF on its adjustment policies. Peru has declared a partial default, no effective action has been taken against her, and none appears likely. Peru not only continues to trade; it is showing signs of a recovery for the first time in a decade and its president enjoys widespread public support—none of which has been lost on other debtors.

The Philippines, Nigeria, Venezuela, and Brazil have also announced or proposed limitations on debt payments. Venezuela and Brazil have opted for "securitization," the conversion into notes or bonds of part of their debt, as had been suggested at the beginning of the crisis by several observers, mainly from the investment banking community. Mexico has been able to virtually eliminate adjustment as the price for new financing, while gaining support for its growth targets and receiving the pledge of a compensatory fund to shield it from commodity price deflation. Other debtors dependent on commodity exports are demanding this last innovation.

Although Mexico may claim a victory of sorts, it has not won the war. But there are clear losers. The IMF and central banks, which safeguard the integrity of the international financial system, have suffered a serious loss of leverage and moral authority. Today, leverage and momentum lie with the debtors. It is not something that the debtors actively sought, but rather something they were driven to by their inability to stimulate economic growth. Governments in debtor countries fighting for their political survival have acted on behalf of their own interests and not on behalf of the integrity of the international financial system. By the same token, executives of commercial banks in the advanced industrial democracies cannot be counted upon to put the interests of international financial stability above their own survival.

The current phase of the debt crisis is one in which the prospects for default have risen while the ability to deter and contain default has diminished. Ultimately, it is the responsibility of the international monetary authorities, the member governments of the OECD, and their central banks to prevent a breakdown in the global financial system. Their authority and their leverage can not be regained, though, unless they recognize the need to correct their diagnosis of what went wrong and their prescription for curing it.

The Remedy

The initial phase of the international debt crisis was widely misdiagnosed as a temporary shortage of liquidity. This diagnosis, based on a set of false or misleading premises, misassessments of the economic cycle, and an ignorance of financial history, led international monetary authorities to prescribe the orthodox medicine for temporary liquidity shortages—domestic austerity and recession, a large surplus in the current account, and additional short-term funding. Years have gone by and the prescription has not worked, except in those few cases (such as Colombia) where the diagnosis was correct. Instead, the old prescription has made the disease worse. Countries structurally unable to handle their debt levels in 1981 and 1982 are that much less able to cope with the substantially higher levels of debt they now have.

The situation is very similar to that of the drug addict who requires ever-larger doses of narcotics, until his system breaks down entirely. But there is a difference. In the debt crisis the doctors themselves have been prescribing and administering successively larger doses of fatal drugs.

There was little enough excuse for the gross errors of analysis committed at the inception of the crisis by the Treasury Department, the IMF, and the major banks (especially Citibank, whose then chairman became notorious for pronouncements such as "countries don't go bankrupt" and "banks don't want to be paid back") as well as by research institutes such as the Institute for International Economics. In 1986 there was no excuse whatsoever, and the underlying rationale of the Baker Plan, of course, belatedly recognizes that the traditional approach to managing the debt crisis is not working.

The diagnosis has changed in the face of reality. What has not changed sufficiently is the subsequent prescription. Appropriate flexibility in administering an effective treatment must include longer-term development funding and the liberalization of the debtor economies (both elements of the Baker Plan). Adding to the debt owed to the commercial banks (on commercial terms) is *not* appropriate and makes the rest of the treatment ineffective. Such action will contribute only to the continued deterioration of the situation. As *The Economist* recently pointed out:

. . . the poorer Mexico gets, the more it will owe. Mr. de la Madrid's predecessor, Mr. Jose Lopez Portillo, borrowed to build vast oil plants and steel mills. All Mr. de la Madrid will have to show is more debt . . . Finance Ministry officials admit. . .that the accord is still a fairly orthodox IMF prescription which, if faithfully adhered to, will ensure a continuing decline in the average worker's purchasing power. This has already fallen by a third since Mr. de la Madrid signed his first IMF agreement three and a half years ago.[2]

Unfortunately, time has been bought only in the short term; ad hoc measures taken to deal with the crisis have not been used to address the real problem in an effective way. The latest Mexican settlement is proof that tactical crisis management—invariably and inappropriately referred to as the "case-by-case" approach—still predominates.

Nevertheless, there are indications that some observers have begun to see the deficiency of the orthodox prescription and the need for a radical new remedy. Several prominent members of the U.S. Congress, led by Senator Bill Bradley of New Jersey, have emphasized that during the first four years of the debt crisis the costs in the creditor countries were absorbed by industry, commerce, agriculture, and labor, not by the banks. Senator Bradley proposed a new debt relief plan involving interest rate reductions, debt write-downs, and new official development loans at an international conference held in Zurich last June. Although hastily conceived and somewhat flawed, Bradley's proposals have already been viewed by the media as an alternative to the Baker Plan, itself a substantial advance over the old prescription.[3]

A remedy to the disease of structural overindebtedness must involve structural reform of the overindebted economy sufficient to relieve the symptoms of overindebtedness. It also must provide debt relief sufficient to permit the overindebted economy to grow without resort to greater fiscal and trade imbalances and, hence, greater indebtedness.

Reducing the economic and political dislocations generated for both debtor and creditor call for additional measures:

• Debtors will need additional long-term development credits to ease the temporary economic and financial dislocations of structural reform;

• Creditors will need greater flexibility in the accounting of their assets and perhaps, in some cases, additional liquidity to reduce the financial burden of providing debt relief;

• If these recommendations are to work, debtors must be shielded from the gravest potential external threat—arbitrary constraint on their export earnings resulting from growing protectionism in the OECD nations.

Based on these principles, Mexico's specific debt problem can be treated in an economically effective and politically feasible fashion. We recommend the following steps.

• *Liberalization and rationalization of the Mexican economy.* As foreshadowed by the Baker Plan, these steps are essential for a successful workout. Measures to increase the levels of domestic savings and capital formation, rationalize the tax system, encourage foreign investment, liberalize trade practices, reduce budget deficits, and cut back overregulation and bureaucratic interference should be adopted as quickly as politically and socially feasible. Without such measures Mexico will continue to face economic and political turmoil.

Admittedly, these measures, if put forward in the absence of other features, would be unacceptable to the Mexican government. It will not risk the short-term economic and, hence, political hardships implicit in structural reform without countervailing concessions. It needs sufficient long-term development funding to relieve the temporary economic dislocations of structural reform and to provide economic and political stability. Without debt relief, Mexico will not enjoy either growth or stability.

• *Increased development funding to aid the liberalization of the Mexican economy.* Given budgetary realities in the developed countries and the limitations of the regional banks, increased development funding for LDCs must come largely from international financial institutions: the regional development banks, the IMF, and particularly the World Bank. In order to increase the resources it can devote to this purpose, the World Bank should call upon its members to pay in a large portion of their authorized capital quotas. Countries that do not comply should have their voting rights reduced.

In addition, the United States and other countries should expand export guarantees and loans to Mexico and other LDCs, and convert official loans to the poorest countries into grants. Such governmental and multilateral assistance should total $8-12 billion per year for at least five years and should be made available to the smaller debtor countries as well as the larger.

• *Debt service limitation based on a flat interest rate, a percent of GDP or GNP, a percent of foreign exchange earnings, or some combination thereof*—sufficient to permit a rate of noninflationary economic growth in Mexico and other structurally overindebted countries of at least 2 percent a year above the rate of population increase. If necessary for regulatory approval, the interest differential may be capitalized (added to the principal of the loan). While the Bradley Plan suggests one way of securing debt relief, we do not believe that a single formula is appropriate for all countries.

Granting debt relief along with our other recommendations represents a general solution to structural overindebtedness and a sufficient incentive for the adoption of domestic reforms. Over time, the application of these proposals would yield lower debt-to-GDP and debt-to-export ratios, suggesting a welcome return to economic health for Mexico and other structurally overindebted economies.

• *Securitization of at least the private portion of Mexico's debt on a long-term, fixed rate basis,* perhaps with interest differential added to the principal of the notes or bonds in the form of final balloon payments. A similar system of convertible securities can be helpful in the privatization of state enterprises. We think that this is a good time for conversion of medium- and long-term debt into securities, since market interest rates are at levels many debtor countries can sustain. The coupon rate on the securities can enable them to be carried initially at par on the banks' books. Securitization has many advantages, including formation of a secondary market in uniform instruments, breaking the absurd myth that all banks are in the same situation and must receive the same treatment, and—most important of all—the fact that as recovery proceeds, Mexico could buy back its own debt at the market discount. Through securitization, banks can limit profit and asset losses, while banks in need of liquidity can secure it.

• *The vigorous application of existing regulatory flexibility to the exposure of U.S. banks in Mexican debt* can enable them to write down their exposure to market in an orderly, long-term fashion. Proper application of Federal Accounting Standard Board Statement No. 15 (FASB 15), for instance, to value-impaired foreign debts would allow banks, under certain conditions, to account for concessions in either principal or interest granted to borrowers' experiencing financial difficulty without requiring the institution to record losses. The use of FASB 15 and other existing accounting procedures would permit the granting of debt relief while limiting the financial damage to the banking system.[4]

• *A halt to any further protectionist measures on the part of the creditors directed against the goods of Mexico (and other debtor countries), and a negotiated rollback of existing barriers.* This should be done on a bilateral basis (although in the context of the new GATT round, the advanced sector has already committed itself to such a policy) so that it can be rapidly implemented. Full reciprocity in trade is appropriate and productive between developed countries; to insist upon full reciprocity between creditor countries and structurally damaged debtor countries will not work, will result in only sterile conflict, and would, in any case, be counterproductive. If the debt-ridden LDCs are able to export relatively freely and qualify for reduced debt service payments, they will be able to—and will—import much more from the creditor countries, thereby easing protectionist pressures.

The Next Phase

The Third World debt crisis has entered a dangerous phase. While political pressures in Mexico and other debtor nations slowly but perceptibly push them toward default, the old solutions to the debt crisis are losing credibility and the political consensus supporting those remedies is disappearing.

We propose a solution the ingredients of which are straightforward. They can be implemented to the benefit of all concerned. But we warn that there is no time for the luxury of either dwelling on assigning blame to others or defending past mistakes. It is, in fact, long past time for a competent diagnosis of the disorder to point the way to an effective remedy.

Mexico is, indeed, a model debtor—not in the sense the term was used in 1983-84, but in the sense that it epitomizes, in exaggerated form, all the elements of the great international debt crisis that erupted in 1981-82. Mexico, like all the structurally impaired debtors, is both a perpetrator and a victim of the crisis. As a perpetrator it has suffered and continues to suffer severely. As a victim, it must have and will have relief—the only question is how that relief will come. Will it come through disruptive and desperate unilateral action? Or will it come through a reasoned and reasonable multilateral settlement? We have perhaps another six to twelve months before this question is answered; perhaps less. Let us begin.

Notes

Chapter 1
1. McNamar's position as chair of the International Monetary Group was known to participants in these meetings, including Dr. Bailey.

Chapter 2
1. Daniel Levy and Gabriel Szekely, *Mexico: Paradoxes of Stability and Change* (Boulder, Colo.: Westview Press, 1983), esp. pp. 126-45, contains a useful discussion of this period.

2. World Bank, *World Development Report 1980*, pp. 156-57.

3. See Vincent L. Padgett, *The Mexican Political System* (Boston: Houghton Mifflin Company, 1976), pp. 306-12, for a detailed analysis of the Echeverria program.

4. See James H. Street, "Mexico's Development Dilemma," *Current History* (December 1983), pp. 411-13.

5. George W. Grayson, "Oil and Politics in Mexico," *Current History* (December 1983), pp. 415-19.

After announcing the discovery of significant petroleum reserves in 1972, the Echeverria government stepped up investments in the hydrocarbon sector, but it was not until 1977, under Lopez Portillo, that a firm decision was made to exploit Mexico's "national treasure," as it was called, as a means of financing fiscal and trade imbalances. The huge expansion of Pemex (the government-owned Mexican petroleum company) from 1977 to 1981 under its director Jorge Diaz Serrano, its immense foreign borrowing, the rapid rise of the petroleum workers' union as a powerful and wealthy national force, and the spread of petro-based corruption put Pemex at the center of Mexican economics and politics. Petroleum production rose from 0.9 million barrels a day in 1977 to 2.25 million in the early 1980s, and before Diaz Serrano was sacked in 1981, he proposed that Mexico produce 4.0 million barrels a day. The impression that Mexico's financial problems could be solved by one commodity gained further credence from 1978-81 as world oil prices rose threefold to over $35 a barrel and, as Lopez Portillo announced in 1981, Mexico discovered new petroleum reserves.

6. Under Echeverria, the Mexican development strategy continued to rest upon "import substitution," seeking to construct a domestic manufacturing sector highly protected from foreign competition which would replace goods currently imported by Mexico. Import substitution had guided Mexico's development strategy since 1940, when the nationalist ideal for the economy was semi-autarky. A central objective of Lopez Portillo's Global Development Plan was to advance the program of import substitution, and his regime continued to support a litany of protectionist policies, including high tariffs and opposition to Mexican entrance into the GATT.

7. Government's role in industry, already large, intensified in the 1970s. When Echeverria entered office, the government was a direct participant in eighty-five enterprises; when he left office, the number had climbed to 845. The total number of workers employed in the public sector doubled from 1970 to 1976, reaching one million. Under Lopez Portillo, the vast expansion of Pemex and accompanying growth of government-run industry in the Global Development Plan ensured a leading role for the state in the economy.

8. After having its interest-to-export ratio decline in 1980 to 70.6 percent from 105.0 percent in 1979 (a result of rising oil prices), the ratio rose to 96.8 percent in 1981, even though the country exported $4.2 billion more in oil that year. Increased income from oil was overwhelmed by a massive increase in interest payments caused by the rise in U.S. interest rates.

9. The drop in oil prices served to slow the growth of Mexico's export earnings. In 1980 oil earnings grew by $6.4 billion; in 1981, by $4.2 billion; and in 1983, by just $2.2 billion.

10. "Capital Flight Fiasco," *The Latin American Times*, no. 73 (June 6, 1986), provides a comprehensive look at the size and impact of capital flight in Latin American economies, including Mexico.

11. The program called for an 8 percent cut in government spending, a reduction of the fiscal deficit from 12.5 percent of GDP to 9.5 percent, absolute limits on foreign borrowing, a rise in domestic interest rates to 55 percent, and a huge cut in construction jobs.

12. Peru's structural imbalance had grown so large relative to national resources that the combination of refinancing and adjustment resulted in a situation in which Peru has not sustained a recovery since 1976. Its real GDP was only 1 percent larger in 1983 than it was in 1975, and its per capita GDP had sharply deteriorated.

Chapter 3

1. During 1983-85 direct foreign investment in Mexico contracted each year, foreign lending to Mexico was strictly involuntary, and domestic investment showed only slight improvement from its devastating collapse in 1983. It is impossible to see why such trends should change suddenly in 1986, especially with domestic demand continuing at depressed levels.

2. Steven E. Sanderson, "Political Tensions in the Mexican Party System," *Current History* (December 1983), provides a short review of the political transformations which evolved in Mexico during the regime of Lopez Portillo.

3. See Padgett, *The Mexican Political System,* pp. 82-84.

4. CTM head Fidel Velasquez's loss of influence was highly visible in 1981 when he supported the unsuccessful candidacy of party bureaucrat Ojeda Paullada to succeed Lopez Portillo during 1981, and when under increasing rank and file pressures, Velasquez moved to escalate intraparty tensions that year, again meeting with no success.

5. John J. Bailey and Donna H. Roberts, "Mexican Agricultural Policy," *Current History* (December 1983). Mexico's agricultural policy initiated in 1980 under the Mexican Food System (SAM) had the objective of reaching food self-sufficiency for Mexico by the mid-1980s. It pursued a recentralization of agricultural land and recapitalization of the agricultural sector. Its land policy served to reduce traditional incentives for peasant support of the government and increased pressures leading toward greater rural unemployment.

6. Echeverria followed a go-slow approach to the tapping of Mexico's hydrocarbon sector while the strong anti-foreigner sentiment within the nationalist left argued for an even more extreme policy of tapping hydrocarbon resources only for domestic use. By 1978 the Lopez Portillo government had rendered the previous debate obsolete: the question had now become how much should Mexico export, and the government rushed to the upper limit.

Chapter 4

1. Peter Field, David Shirrett, and William Ollard, "The IMF and Central Banks Flex Their Muscles," *Euromoney* (January 1983), provides a full account of the pivotal role of the IMF and the Federal Reserve in organizing creditor unity following the Mexican payments crisis of 1981.

2. Erik Ipsen, "After Mexico, the Regionals Are in Retreat," *Euromoney* (January 1983), defines the principal differences between the objectives and interests of U.S. regional banks and the U.S. money center banks.

3. Alan Robinson, "Portillo Pockets the Banks," *Euromoney* (October

1982), outlines the events surrounding Lopez Portillo's decision to nationalize the banks and provides some useful information on the pedigrees
of key figures in the nationalist left.

4. Carlos Tello, who was a student of Flores de la Pena (a prominent
figure in the Echeverria government), had espoused a policy of fast industrialization, enlarged protectionism, and more public ownership of
industry and the banks. Tello had co-authored a book with Rolando Cor-
dera, the leading public opponent of petroleum exploitation for export
and the head, in 1982, of the parliamentary contingent of the electoral
leftist party, the PSUM (Partido Socialista Unificado de Mexico). In
his book, Tello argued for greater protectionism, nationalization of key
industries, greater control of the private sector (especially the banks),
lower interest rates, and large government investment programs.

5. Silva Herzog tendered his resignation immediately in the aftermath
of the bank nationalization announcement and was joined by orthodox
cohorts in the cabinet, Miguel Mancera, director of the Bank of Mexico, and Adrian Lajous, head of the Banco de Comercio Exterior. Only
Silva Herzog's resignation was rejected by Lopez Portillo.

6. The critical point of difference between the Mexican government
and the IMF in the fall 1982 negotiations centered about Mexico's fiscal
deficit. In 1982 the fiscal deficit reached 17.6 percent of GDP. The initial Mexican government offer was to reduce the fiscal deficit in 1983
to 14-15 percent of GDP. The IMF, on the other hand, pushed for the
fiscal deficit to be reduced to 6 percent of GDP. In the November settlement Mexico agreed to reduce its deficit to 8.5 percent of GDP in
1983, marking a clear victory for the IMF. In addition, the government
was to reduce its 1984 fiscal deficit to 5.5 percent of GDP and its 1985
deficit to 3.5 percent. Strict limits were placed on money supply growth,
and inflation was targeted to be brought down to 55 percent in 1983 from
nearly 100 percent in 1982.

7. *IMF Report on Mexico,* January 1984.

8. In 1985 agreement was reached with Mexico's creditors for a restructuring of $48.7 billion of foreign debt. After completion of the first tranche
of the agreement, Silva Herzog called it a "fundamental step on the road
of combined efforts directed at Mexico's debt problem which will permit an early return to voluntary financing markets." The first tranche
of the agreement covered $23.6 billion in medium-term credits agreed
to by Mexico's creditors in March 1983. The second tranche agreed to
in August 1985 involved $20.1 billion of debt of thirty-six public bor-
rowers due between 1985 and 1990.

Chapter 5

1. Jorge G. Castaneda, "Mexico at the Brink," *Foreign Affairs* (Winter 1985/86), reviews the growing political isolation of the Mexican government and the rise of middle-class resentment.

2. The PAN won mayoralty races in key cities including Chihuahua, Juarez, Durango, Hermosillo (the capital of Sonora), and Obregon (which dominates Mexico's breadbasket in the Yaqui and Mayo valleys).

3. The PRI candidate won only 55 percent of the vote, 10 percent below the PRI national average, in seven of Mexico's eight most populous and prosperous states which comprise 42 percent of the registered voters. With vote fraud calculated to have averaged 10 percent nationwide, the PRI's real vote in these states was probably closer to 45 percent.

4. Delal M. Baer, "The 1986 Mexican Elections: The Case of Chihuahua," Latin American Study Series, Report No. 1, Center for Strategic and International Studies, Washington, D.C., September 1986, p. 35.

5. Robert J. McCartney, "New Loans to Mexico in Doubt," *The Washington Post* (September 1985).

6. "New Shock Bid to Curb Crisis," *Latin America Weekly Report* (December 13, 1985).

7. The 1986 Mexican budget was padded. The budget forecast only a $2 a barrel price drop for petroleum in 1986, at least $3 a barrel less than most experts were predicting in late 1985. Also, the budget estimated 10 percent growth in Mexico's non-oil exports, even though such exports had contracted by 10 percent in 1985 and world markets in 1986 were not expected to expand.

8. The Mexican government had forecast 1986 exports to reach $22.6 billion. However, at $15 a barrel average price for Mexican oil and at production levels of 1.5 million barrels a day, the country would lose $6.24 billion in 1986 export earnings. With Mexican crude oil prices averaging well below $15 a barrel and production slipping to 1.1 million barrels a day, Mexico will lose $8 billion from 1985 earnings and $7 billion from 1986 budget projections. Thus, Mexico's exports will fall to $15.6 billion in 1986 as a result of the oil price collapse, and its trade surplus will not be the anticipated $9.6 billion, but only $2.6 billion. In order to pay its bills, therefore, Mexico will need, in addition to the $4 billion it had originally asked for, another $7 billion. Because of lower world interest rates, however, combined with a strengthening tourist trade, Mexico needs about $4-5 billion more than its original request. If imports are further retrenched, this figure could be brought down to $3-4 billion. Thus, for 1986 Mexico's borrowing needs were about $7-8 billion.

9. Revenue losses from the collapse of oil earnings were expected to be in the range of 12.5-15.0 percent of anticipated revenues, making Mex-

ico's fiscal deficit for 1986 more than 10 percent of GDP. Inflation has already begun to soar; it reached 13.2 percent in January and February (equivalent to 80 percent on an annual basis) and accelerated during the summer months.

10. In February Silva Herzog traveled to Washington where he met with Volcker and Baker and received no sympathy for Mexico's requests. He visited Washington again in March, and again was told that Mexico would have to make significant sacrifices to adjustment. In April formal negotiations with the IMF were resumed.

11. "The Peso Collapses on Moratorium Tip," *Latin American Weekly Report* (June 13, 1986).

12. James Rowe, Jr., "Reagan Vows U.S. Help to Mexico," *The Washington Post* (June 12, 1986). President Reagan was called on to act during this period, delivering an appeal to Mexico in one of his televised press conferences.

13. Aside from its impact on the presidential succession in Mexico, the removal of Silva Herzog was perceived to mean a shift in Mexico's negotiating style. Whereas Silva Herzog would seek creditor reactions to proposed Mexican policies before acting, Mexico would now act first and ask questions later.

14. "Mexican Threat to Stop Paying Led to IMF Pact," *The Washington Post* (August 3, 1986).

Chapter 6

1. Between 1986 and 1988 the Mexican economy will grow at an annual average rate of less than 1.0 percent if the government's target, supported by the IMF, of 3.5-4.0 percent growth actually materializes in 1987-88 because the Mexican economy will contract by 4.0-5.0 percent during 1986. By the end of 1988 the Mexican GDP in real terms will be only 2.3 percent larger than it was at the end of 1985. At the same time, Mexico's foreign debt will grow by a minimum of $12 billion, or 12 percent, between 1986-88 if the Mexico-IMF agreement is supported by Mexico's private creditors. If oil prices remain at present levels, Mexico will need additional funds in 1988. Thus, Mexico's foreign debt will grow by $12-20 billion from 1986 to 1988, or 12-20 percent. As a result, the nation's overindebtedness problem will worsen over the next three years as the debt-to-GDP ratio grows.

2. Mexico's inflation rate as of mid-year was quickly reaching the 100 percent level for 1986, up from the 65 percent inflation rate registered at the end of 1985. The $12 billion in new money targeted for Mexico in 1986-87 as a result of the IMF-Mexico deal would largely go to make up revenue shortfalls derived from the collapse of oil prices. Mexico's underlying growth potential for 1987-88, as projected by the British econometric service IEAS, is -1.8 to 0.45 percent. Mexico will therefore

have to maintain hefty fiscal deficits in 1987-88 if it wishes to reach its growth target. Large fiscal deficits will force the government to relax money supply and allow domestic interest rates to fall; otherwise, government borrowing would crowd out private borrowing and depress private investment and consumption, thereby bringing GDP below 3.5-4.0 percent. Thus, to sustain 3.5-4.0 percent growth in 1987-88, Mexico will have to accept high inflation and lower interest rates. Such circumstances will spur capital flight and new payments problems.

3. *The Economist* (August 9, 1986), p. 27.

4. The following excerpts from the testimony of Comptroller of the Currency Robert L. Clarke before the U.S. Senate Committee on Banking, Housing, and Urban Affairs, March 11, 1986, indicate the degree of flexibility which exists and which the regulators have encouraged the banks to use with reference to certain categories of domestic debt:

> It is our view that the most beneficial thing we can do for those [agricultural] banks and their borrowers is to ensure that they have the opportunity and incentive to work with their borrowers to achieve mutually satisfactory loan workout plans. In particular, we must identify and remove obstacles that inhibit banks from successfully helping themselves and their borrowers. It is only by identifying their losses and restructuring credits to reduce farmers' debt burdens, that agricultural banks will be able to put their problems behind them and improve the quality of their loan portfolios. . . .
>
> The three federal bank regulatory agencies have been considering for some time a variety of ways that banks could be given the tools and the encouragement to effect long-term restructuring of problem credits. Among the options are the following, *none of which require legislative action and all of which could be implemented by regulatory decisions* [emphasis added].
>
> First, banks could be encouraged to understand and use the provisions of Financial Accounting Standards Board Statement No. 15 (FASB 15) to account for restructured debt. FASB 15 can, under certain circumstances, be used to account for concessions in financing terms (i.e., reduction of either principal or interest) granted to borrowers experiencing financial difficulty without requiring the institution to record any losses. FASB 15 has not been readily used in the past. *Many bankers simply have not been aware of its existence. . . .* [emphasis added]. An example of how it would work follows:
>
> *FASB 15*
> Assume that a farmer has borrowed $100,000 at 12 percent for five years. Using a straight-line amortization schedule and simple interest, the farmer's payments would total $136,000 over the five-

year term. Assume the borrower's cash flow drops so that he can no longer afford to pay the entire amount over the five-year term. To accommodate this reduction in cash flow, the lender can restructure the loan by extending the maturity, foregoing principal, reducing the interest rate, or some combination of the three. As long as the total cash payments to the lender aggregate to $100,000, the original amount of the loan, and the restructuring is done based upon reasonable prospects for repayment, under FASB 15, the lender would not have to write down the loan and recognize losses.

Second, we would propose modification of the present call report disclosure requirements for restructured loans to allow banks to distinguish those loans that, although restructured, are in compliance with the new terms. *Under this proposal, such restructured loans would no longer be included in the category of nonperforming loans* [emphasis added]. Such a change would require a revision in the call report, which we are prepared to initiate immediately.

Third, and perhaps most importantly, we are considering the option of capital forbearance that *we believe will encourage banks to write down problem loans and develop workout plans* [emphasis added]. The essence of this option is to encourage agricultural banks to recognize losses, but allow them to operate temporarily with lower levels of capital. Because a primary purpose of capital is to absorb unanticipated losses, we believe that agricultural banks should now take advantage of their traditionally high levels of capital.

Capital forbearance, which is really a variation on loan loss deferral plans—but a better one we think—would permit banks to place a portion of their agricultural loan chargeoffs into a segregated account. The amount in the segregated account could not exceed some percent of the bank's primary capital. Additions to the segregated account could be made during the first two years after implementation of the policy. The segregated account would then be amortized in equal increments during the five years immediately following the addition to the segregated account. Thus, the segregated account would exist for a maximum of seven years. An example of how this option could be utilized follows:

Capital Forbearance
Assume that an agricultural bank with $50 million in assets and $5 million in capital incurs loan losses of $1 million. Under our present rules, the loans would be charged off against the loan loss reserve which the bank is required to maintain. Because the reserve is permitted to be included in primary capital, the $1 million charge

against the reserve would reduce the bank's capital by $1 million. Under the capital forbearance option, the $1 million in agricultural loan losses would be placed in a segregated account and included as a memorandum account for reporting purposes. The segregated account would be reduced by $200,000 per year over the following five years. . . .

Capital forbearance would have other benefits as well. It would set simple limits to give agricultural banks a clear understanding of the regulatory concession. Agricultural banks could easily calculate their losses and resulting capital position. Moreover, write-downs taken to qualify loans for the FmHA guarantee could reduce the amount of classified assets, thereby improving the quality of a bank's remaining loan portfolio. Also, by encouraging banks to make legitimate chargeoffs, it could enable them to reduce their tax bill or recover previously paid taxes.

There are also administrative advantages to this option. It requires no statutory change. Although it initially specifies a seven-year timeframe, we would have the flexibility to extend it if conditions so warrant. It is easily understandable and self-executing, which means that bankers can enjoy the benefits immediately rather than make an application to the regulator and wait for a response. Finally, it utilizes existing programs and would not represent significant increased resource costs to the banking agencies.